Wiener Urtext Edition

UT 50408

Franz Schubert

Impromptus op. 90 (D 899)

Nach den Quellen herausgegeben von Ulrich Leisinger
Hinweise zur Interpretation von Robert D. Levin
Fingersätze von Paul Badura-Skoda

Edited from the sources by Ulrich Leisinger
Notes on Interpretation by Robert D. Levin
Fingering by Paul Badura-Skoda

Edité d'après les sources par Ulrich Leisinger
Notes sur l'interprétation de Robert D. Levin
Doigté de Paul Badura-Skoda

Wiener Urtext Edition, Schott/Universal Edition

Wiener Urtext Edition, Musikverlag Ges. m. b. H. & Co., K. G., Wien
Ein Gemeinschaftsunternehmen der Verlage Schott Music GmbH & Co. KG, Mainz und Universal Edition, Wien

© 2015 by Wiener Urtext Edition, Musikverlag Ges. m. b. H. & Co., K. G., Wien

ISMN 979-0-50057-394-4

INHALT / CONTENTS / CONTENU

Vorwort III
Hinweise zur Interpretation IV
Preface... V
Notes on Interpretation................................... VI
Préface VIII
Notes sur l'interprétation IX

Facsimilia... 11, 29

4 Impromptus op. 90 (D 899)

Impromptu in c op. 90/1 (D 899/1)

Impromptu in Es op. 90/2 (D 899/2)

Impromptu in Ges op. 90/3 (D 899/3)

Impromptu in As op. 90/4 (D 899/4)

Kritische Anmerkungen 40
Critical Notes........................... 43

VORWORT

Franz Schuberts *Vier Impromptus* op. 90 bilden die erste Serie von insgesamt acht *Impromptus*, die als Opus 90 und Opus 142 des Komponisten bekannt geworden sind. Das genaue Entstehungsdatum ist nicht bekannt, doch dürften die Stücke aus einer Reihe von Gründen in die Mitte des Jahres 1827 fallen. Zu Schuberts Lebzeiten sind nur die beiden ersten Stücke aus op. 90 bei Tobias Haslinger in Wien gedruckt worden. Ihr Erscheinen ist noch mit der abweichenden Opuszahl 87 in der *Wiener Zeitung* vom 10. Dezember 1827 angezeigt. Unklar bleibt, warum die beiden Impromptus op. 90/3 und op. 90/4 erst lange nach Schuberts Tod gedruckt wurden. Das Autograph hat Tobias Haslinger (1787–1842) noch selbst für den Druck eingerichtet, doch sind die Stücke erst 15 Jahre nach dem Tod des Verlegers durch dessen Sohn Carl veröffentlicht worden. Dabei betrachtete man es offenbar als Erleichterung für den Spieler, in op. 90/3 Schuberts Großtakte im 4/2-Takt in einen 2/2-Takt zu unterteilen und das Stück von Ges-Dur nach G-Dur zu transponieren. In dieser Form war das Stück bis zur Mitte des 20. Jahrhunderts allgemein bekannt, obwohl es bereits in der *Alten Schubert-Gesamtausgabe* (1888) in der Originaltonart gedruckt worden war. Durch die Untergliederung der Großtakte droht aber der natürliche Fluss verloren zu gehen, und die Transposition ist zwar eine lesetechnische, aber keine spieltechnische Erleichterung, denn Schuberts Stück liegt in Ges-Dur sehr bequem in der Hand.

Für den Titel „Impromptu" finden sich um 1820 mehrere Vorbilder. Häufig wird auf die sechs *Impromptus* op. 7 von Jan Václav Voříšek verwiesen, die 1822 bei Pietro Mechetti in Wien erschienen sind. Aber auch von anderen namhaften Komponisten wie Johann Baptist Cramer, Carl Czerny, Heinrich Marschner, Ignaz Moscheles oder dem jungen Franz Liszt finden sich um diese Zeit gedruckte Impromptus. Als literaturhistorischer Begriff meint „Impromptu" dem Wortsinne nach ein Gedicht aus dem Stehgreif; dieser improvisatorische Zug schwingt beispielsweise in verschiedenen Werken von Johann Baptist Cramer sowie in Franz Liszts Opus 3, einem *Impromptu brillant sur des Thêmes de Rossini et Spontini*, mit. Für Schuberts klar strukturierte Impromptus trifft diese Gestaltungsweise mit Ausnahme des ersten Stücks aus Opus 90, das sich in entwickelnder Variation aus einem viertaktigen Gedanken entfaltet, nicht zu. Opus 90/2–4 sind architektonisch klar strukturierte Stücke in dreiteiliger Form, die teils durch eine Coda beschlossen werden.

Schuberts *Impromptus* op. 90 sind im Autograph überliefert. Für Opus 90/1 gibt es zusätzlich einen ersten autographen Entwurf. Das vollständige Autograph dient der vorliegenden Ausgabe als Hauptquelle, die Erstausgaben wurden als Nebenquellen berücksichtigt. Von den *Impromptus* op. 90 gibt es nur wenige zeitgenössische Abschriften. Die wichtigsten sind die Abschriften der *Impromptus* op. 90/3 und 4 in der Sammlung Witteczek-Spaun, die seit 1865 im Archiv der Gesellschaft der Musikfreunde in Wien aufbewahrt wird. Die Abschriften dieser Sammlung folgen den Autographen getreu, weisen aber gelegentlich zusätzliche Artikulationsangaben auf, die sich als sinnvolle Fortsetzung der von Schubert festgelegten Prinzipien erweisen und daher nicht von vornherein ignoriert werden dürfen.

Schuberts Autograph ist ohne größere Schwierigkeiten lesbar. Die Tonhöhen und rhythmischen Werte sind deutlich zu erkennen, bei der Setzung der Akzidentien ist Schubert mitunter aber nachlässig. Dynamische Angaben werden meist bereits vor den gemeinten Noten gesetzt, was in den Erstdrucken gelegentlich zu Irrtümern führt. Artikulationszeichen sind gerne zwischen den Systemen platziert, wobei nicht immer eindeutig zu erkennen ist, ob sie auch tatsächlich für beide Systeme gelten sollen. Schwierigkeiten bereitet auch die Bogensetzung, da die Position der Bögen häufig ungenau ist. Die Artikulation erscheint selten ganz ausgefeilt. Wenn ein Artikulationsmodell eingeführt wird, hat Schubert dies oft nur wenige Male im Detail notiert. Im weiteren Verlauf kann die Artikulation nachlässiger werden oder im Sinne eines *simile* ganz fehlen. Der Blick auf Parallelstellen führt in vielen Fällen nicht weiter, da sie häufig in Details abweichen, wobei unklar bleibt, ob Schubert die Änderungen willentlich vorgenommen hat oder ob sie nur zufällig entstanden sind.

Zwei Besonderheiten von Schuberts Notation seien noch eigens erwähnt, der Gebrauch des Akzentzeichens sowie die Variabilität bei der Notierung von Artikulationspunkten und -strichen. Schuberts Autographe erhalten durch den üppigen Gebrauch von Akzentzeichen ein charakteristisches Aussehen. Manchmal sind breit gezogene Akzentzeichen von Decrescendo-Gabeln nicht eindeutig zu unterscheiden. In der vorliegenden Neuausgabe wurden Akzente nur bevorzugt, wenn nicht im unmittelbaren Kontext auch Crescendo-Gabeln stehen, zu denen ein Decrescendo korrespondieren würde. Sofern Schubert nicht sehr flüchtig schreibt, besteht ein deutlicher Unterschied zwischen Artikulationspunkten und Artikulationsstrichen. Die Wahl ergibt sich in erster Linie aus dem dynamischen Kontext: Im Piano setzt Schubert fast ausschließlich Punkte, im Forte hingegen eher Striche. Bei Portato-Stellen ist mitunter zu beobachten, dass die Punkte suggestiv dem Spieltempo angepasst werden. Im Autograph des *Impromptus* in Ges op. 90/3 sind die Portato-Punkte daher sehr breit gezogen und nähern sich mitunter fast schon Tenuto-Strichen an; in den zeitgenössischen Abschriften und im Erstdruck wird diese Unterscheidung aber nicht weiter beachtet.

Die vorliegende Neuausgabe folgt Schuberts Autograph als Hauptquelle. Ergänzungen aus Nebenquellen stehen im Notentext in runden Klammern. Hinzufügungen aus den handschriftlichen Nebenquellen sind zudem in den Einzelanmerkungen ausgewiesen. Herausgeberzutaten wurden durch eckige Klammern gekennzeichnet.

Ulrich Leisinger

HINWEISE ZUR INTERPRETATION[1]

Ausführung und Ausdruck

Bei allen Aspekten der Aufführungspraxis ist es entscheidend, zwischen Ausführung – den generellen aufführungspraktischen Regeln der Zeit unabhängig von der spezifischen Eigenart einer Stelle – und dem Ausdruck, der direkt mit dem erlebbaren Charakter einer Passage in Verbindung steht, zu unterscheiden. So könnte zum Beispiel im *Impromptu* in c-Moll op. 90/1 die Ausführung des stets gleich notierten punktierten Rhythmus ♪.♬ gemäß den in der Abfolge unterschiedlichen Charakteren variieren:

Takt 1ff.: eine relativ exakte rhythmische Ausführung innerhalb der Legato-Linie;
Takt 5ff.: eine leicht überpunktierte Ausführung mit einer etwas später und kürzer gespielten Sechzehntelnote als bei einer notenwertgetreuen Ausführung in Übereinstimmung mit dem marschartigen Charakter der Stelle;
Takt 41ff.: an den Rhythmus der Triolen angeglichen angesichts der ausdrucksvollen Cantabile-Melodie (siehe dazu zur Ausführung punktierter Rhythmen weiter unten).

Dynamik

Schubert schreibt einen Dynamikbereich von *fff* bis *ppp* sowie die Sforzato-Symbole *fp*, *fz* und *ffz* vor (*sf* scheint in diesen Stücken nicht auf). Es ist wahrscheinlich, dass bei Wiener Klavieren, die vor etwa 1840 gebaut wurden, *ppp* die Verwendung des Harfenzugs (Moderator) meint. Daneben fordert Schubert gelegentlich das *una corda*-Pedal („Mit Verschiebung"). Aus diesem Grund dürfte es schon auf einem Wiener Klavier unklug sein, die Verschiebung bei jedem Auftreten von *pp* einzusetzen; und besonders auf modernen Klavieren ist hiervon dringend abzuraten, da sonst die besonders zarten Passagen im *ppp* klanglich nicht von denen im *pp* zu unterscheiden sind.

Decrescendo und Diminuendo

Schubert unterscheidet in der Regel zwischen *ritardando* (langsamer werden), *decrescendo* (leiser werden) und *diminuendo* (leiser und langsamer werden). Zwar wurde diese Differenzierung gelegentlich in Frage gestellt, aber sie wird durch eine Reihe von Beobachtungen gestützt: Erstens: Im Gegensatz zu Beethoven, der *decrescendo* in seinen früheren Werken verwendete, aber sich in seinen späteren Kompositionen auf *diminuendo* verlegte, benutzt Schubert während seiner gesamten Schaffenszeit die beiden Begriffe nebeneinander in ein und demselben Satz. Offenkundig gibt es keinen philologischen Vorteil für die Verwendung von zwei gegeneinander austauschbaren Begriffen, wenn sie wirklich dasselbe bedeuten sollen. Zweitens: Nach *diminuendo* trifft man häufig auf ein *a tempo*. *A tempo* kommt hingegen nie nach *decrescendo* vor. Und drittens: Es lässt sich mit einem hohen Maß an Wahrscheinlichkeit vorhersagen, wann und wo ein *diminuendo* auftritt, und zwar am Ende der Exposition und der Reprise, in der Coda oder in der Rückleitung zur Reprise, also an Stellen mit überleitendem oder schließendem Charakter.

Artikulation

Die Klarheit der Artikulation, durch die sich die Wiener Klaviere auszeichnen, ist ein zentrales Kennzeichen des klassischen Stils. Als die Klaviere klangstärker wurden und damit auch länger nachklangen, wurden die Bögen länger und die Artikulationsangaben weniger detailliert. Im Verlaufe seines Schaffens verwendete Beethoven Bögen und Artikulationszeichen immer mehr, um nicht nur die vorgesehene Ausführung seiner Musik, sondern auch ihre Form und Richtung anzuzeigen. Schubert war, wie die meisten seiner Zeitgenossen, von Beethovens Innovationen in diesem Bereich beeinflusst; wie Beethoven verwendet er den Begriff *ligato* (nicht *legato*) mit gewisser Regelmäßigkeit, während im 18. Jahrhundert ein Non-Legato die Regel war und Legato als expressive Wirkung eingesetzt wurde. Schuberts Artikulationsangaben spiegeln dennoch zu einem gewissen Grad auch noch die Tonsprache Mozarts und Haydns wider. So werden Töne ohne Artikulationszeichen normalerweise voneinander abgesetzt gespielt, wobei der Grad des Absetzens vom Ausdrucksgehalt abhängt.

Nach der Violinschule von Leopold Mozart und anderen zeitgenössischen Traktaten zeigen Bögen nicht nur ein Legatospiel an, sondern sind auch als ein Decrescendo zu verstehen, wobei die letzte Note in der Regel leichter zu spielen ist[2]. Diese Praxis behielt auch für das ganze 19. Jahrhundert ihre Gültigkeit; Augenzeugen bestätigen, dass noch Brahms so phrasiert hat. Wie bei Mozart und Haydn, sollte der Bass-Ton über die ganze Gruppe hinweg liegenbleiben, wenn Alberti-Bässe und andere verwandte Figuren in der Klaviermusik mit Bögen versehen sind (Fingerpedal).

Punktierte Rhythmen

Von der Barockzeit bis ins frühe 20. Jahrhundert war es üblich, den Triolenrhythmus lang-kurz (♩♪ mit 3) bei Passagen mit Triolen als ♪.♬ zu notieren, wobei die Sechzehntelnote gemeinsam mit dem letzten Triolenachtel erklang. Nur bei langsamem Tempo wurde von dieser Konvention abgewichen und die Sechzehntel nach dem dritten Triolenachtel gespielt[3]. Dies könnte angesichts der Tempobezeichnung *Allegro molto moderato* auch für das *c-Moll-Impromptu*, op. 90/1 gelten, wenn der Hauptakzent der Tempoangabe auf *molto moderato* liegt. Es ist aber notwendig, darauf hinzuweisen, dass sowohl in Schuberts Autograph als auch im Erstdruck die Sechzehntelnote beim Rhythmus ♪.♬ mit der dritten Triolenachtel zusammenfällt. Wenn überhaupt, so steht die Sechzehntelnote geringfügig vor dem letzten Achtel einer Triole, aber nie danach. Aus diesem Grund werden in der vorliegenden Ausgabe Punktierungen und Triolen aneinander angeglichen.

Verzierungen

Bis weit ins 19. Jahrhundert wurden Triller mit der oberen Nebennote begonnen und Vorschlagsnoten auf dem Schlag gespielt. Chopin wandte die Trillerausführung „von oben" während seiner gesamten Lebenszeit an. Dennoch kamen im 18. Jahrhundert auch Ausnahmen von dieser Regel auf, und Schuberts Lebenszeit war eine Zeit des Übergangs. Triller von der Hauptnote sind in erster Linie dann zu verwenden, wenn sie zu einem natürlicheren Melodieverlauf führen, beispielsweise dann, wenn ihnen ein rascher Lauf abwärts oder aufwärts unmittelbar vorangeht und der Trillerbeginn von oben zu einem ungewöhnlichen Sprung oder zu einer Tonwiederholung führen würde. Schubert notiert Nachschläge bei den Trillern nicht immer, obwohl diese bis mindestens zur Mitte des 19. Jahrhunderts als Standard anzusehen sind. Zwar gibt es gelegentlich Fälle, in denen auf Nachschläge verzichtet werden kann, vor allem bei höherem Tempo und bei Trillern auf kurzen Noten; dies ist jedoch eher die Ausnahme als die Regel.

Pedalgebrauch

Schubert schreibt die Verwendung des (rechten) Pedals nur ganz selten explizit vor. Es ist jedoch wahrscheinlich, dass Schubert mit häufigerer Verwendung des Pedals zur Aufhebung der Dämpfung rechnete[4]. Grundsätzlich sind Abschnitte mit langsamem harmonischen Rhythmus, in denen nur wenige Sekundfortschreitungen vorkommen, für die Verwendung des Pedals gut geeignet; die Verwendung des Pedals ist selbst dann nicht ausgeschlossen, wenn zum Beispiel die erste Note einer Figur in der linken Hand einen Staccato-Punkt oder Artikulationsstrich aufweist. Auf der anderen Seite erlaubt der hellere, klarere Klang der Wiener Klaviere der Schubert-Zeit einen sparsameren Pedalgebrauch, als er auf heutigen Instrumenten üblich ist.

Bemerkungen zu den einzelnen Werken

Impromptu op. 90/1

Die Ornamente ♫ (Takt 19) und ↯ (Takt 26 und 181) sind vor dem Schlag zu spielen; zu beachten ist dabei, dass eine Ausführung auf dem Schlag in Takt 19 zu Oktavparallelen mit dem Bass führen und dabei gleichzeitig einen Dissonanzton (*c*) verdoppeln würde, anstatt den verminderten Septakkord vollständig darzustellen.

In Takt 75/76 und an den Parallelstellen ist sowohl eine Ausführung der Vorschläge vor wie auf der Zeit möglich; erstere wirkt eleganter, vgl. dazu Takt 79/80, wo die Halbenote ausdrücklich auf dem Schlag steht.

Der Vorhalt in Takt 107, der eine Dissonanz mit Akzent ist, muss auf dem Schlag ausgeführt werden, da sonst parallele Quinten zwischen den Oberstimmen entstehen.

Impromptu op. 90/3

Die Appoggiatur in der linken Hand in Takt 75 scheint anzuzeigen, dass der Triller mit der oberen Note (*eses*) begonnen werden soll.

Robert D. Levin
(Deutsche Übersetzung Ulrich Leisinger)

---

[1] Für Anregungen und Hinweise bei der Vorbereitung dieser Interpretationshinweise danke ich Malcolm Bilson.
[2] Leopold Mozart, *Versuch einer gründlichen Violinschule*, Augsburg 1756, S. 135.
[3] Vgl. hierzu Carl Czerny zum ersten Satz der *Mondschein-Sonate* von Beethoven in: *Über den richtigen Vortrag der sämtlichen Beethoven'schen Klavierwerke*, in: *Vollständige theoretisch-practische Pianoforte-Schule op. 500*, Bd. 4, Kapitel 2 und 3, hg. und kommentiert von Paul Badura-Skoda, Wien 1970, S. 51: *Die Sechzehntel ist der untern letzten Triolen_Note nachzuschlagen ...*
[4] Siehe dazu im Allgemeinen: David Rowland, *A History of Pianoforte Pedalling*, Cambridge 1993.

PREFACE

Franz Schubert's *Four Impromptus* Op. 90 constitute the first series of his total of eight *Impromptus* Op. 90 and Op. 142. It is not known when exactly the pieces were written, but for a number of reasons this was probably around the middle of the year 1827. In Schubert's lifetime only the first two pieces of opus 90 appeared in print in an edition by Tobias Haslinger. Their publication is announced in the *Wiener Zeitung* on 10 December 1827 with the deviating opus number 87. What remains unclear is why the two *Impromptus* Op. 90/3 and Op. 90/4 weren't published until long after Schubert's death. Tobias Haslinger (1787–1842) had personally prepared the autograph for printing, but the pieces were published only 15 years after the publisher's death by his son Carl. Obviously it was considered a facilitation for the performer to divide Schubert's double bars in 4/2 time in opus 90/3 into bars in 2/2 time and transpose the piece from G flat major to G major. It was in this form that the piece was known until the middle of the 20th century, even though it had already been printed in the original key in the *Alte Schubert-Gesamtausgabe* (1888). But in dividing the 4/2 bars the natural flow is lost and the transposition may be a facilitation for reading but not for playing, since Schubert's piece lies very comfortably under the fingers in G flat.

We can find several models for the title of *Impromptu* around 1820. The six *Impromptus* Op. 7 by Jan Václav Voříšek published in 1822 by Pietro Mechetti in Vienna are often mentioned in this context.

But also renowned composers such as Johann Baptist Cramer, Carl Czerny, Heinrich Marschner, Ignaz Moscheles or the young Franz Liszt wrote Impromptus that were published around this time. As a literary term, 'impromptu' signifies a poem created on the spur of the moment; this improvisational trait is audible for instance in various works by Johann Baptist Cramer as well as in Franz Liszt's opus 3, an *Impromptu brillant sur des Thèmes de Rossini et Spontini*. This pattern however does not apply to Schubert's clearly structured *Impromptus*, perhaps with the exception of the first piece of opus 90 that unfolds in a developing variation from a 4-bar idea. In opus 90, architectonically clearly structured pieces in tripartite form predominate, some of them ending with a coda.

For the *Impromptus* Op. 90 Schubert's autograph has completely survived, for opus 90/1 additionally a first draft is extant. For the present edition the autograph serves as principal source; the first editions have been considered as secondary sources. There are only a few contemporary copies of the *Impromptus* Op. 90. The most important ones are the manuscript copies of Opp. 90/3 and 90/4 in the collection of Witteczek-Spaun, which is preserved since 1865 in the archive of the *Gesellschaft der Musikfreunde* in Vienna. These copies faithfully follow the autograph, but occasionally show additional articulation marks that constitute a sensible continuation of the principles laid down by Schubert and should therefore not be ignored out of hand.

Schubert's autograph can be read without too much trouble. The pitches and rhythmic values can be clearly identified. But when placing accidentals Schubert tends to be somewhat careless. Dynamic marks are often notated already before the notes they refer to, which has led to occasional errors in the first editions. Articulation marks are often placed between the staves, so it is not always clear whether they indeed apply to both staves. The placing of slurs also presents problems, since the position of the slurs is often inaccurate. Articulation is rarely written out in detail. When an articulation pattern is introduced Schubert only notates this a few times in a detailed manner. Subsequently, articulation can become more careless or disappear altogether in the sense of a *simile*. In many cases cross-checking parallel passages is of little help, since they often diverge in their details, leaving unclear whether Schubert made the changes consciously or whether they came about by chance.

Two peculiarities of Schubert's notation should be mentioned here, the use of the accent mark as well as the variability in notating articulation dots and strokes. The ample use of accent marks gives Schubert's autographs a characteristic appearance. Sometimes elongated accent marks cannot be clearly distinguished from decrescendo hairpins. The present edition only favours accents provided there are no crescendo hairpins in the immediate vicinity that would call for a corresponding decrescendo. Provided Schubert does not write very hastily there is a clear difference between articulation dots and articulation strokes. The choice depends primarily on the dynamic context: In *piano* Schubert notates almost exclusively dots, in *forte* preferably strokes. In *portato* passages one can also sometimes observe that the dots are adjusted suggestively to the playing tempo. In the autograph of the *Impromptu* in G flat major Op. 90/3 the *portato* dots are therefore drawn out very broadly and almost take the form of *tenuto* dashes; in the contemporary copies and in the first edition this differentiation is however ignored.

For the present edition Schubert's autograph has been used as the principal source. Additions that originate from secondary sources are always indicated in parentheses in the musical text. Additions from secondary manuscript sources are furthermore mentioned in the detailed notes. Additions by the editor are indicated by square brackets.

Ulrich Leisinger
(Translation Matthias Müller)

NOTES ON INTERPRETATION[1]

Execution and Expression

In all matters of performance, it is crucial to distinguish between execution – the general performance principles of the time without regard to the specific character of a given passage – and expression, which is directly connected with the perceived character. All of the details discussed below should be understood in this context. For example, in the *Impromptu* in C minor, Op. 90/1, the dotted rhythm might best vary in execution according to the different successive characters:

at bars 1ff. with relatively exact execution within the legato line;

at bars 5ff. with the semiquaver (sixteenth note) in the dotted rhythm slightly later and shorter than literal execution, in keeping with the march character;

at bars 41ff. aligned with the triplet given the expressive cantabile melody (see Execution of Dotted Rhythms below)

Dynamics

Schubert prescribes a dynamic range from *fff* to *ppp* as well as the accentuation and *sforzato* symbols *fp*, *fz* and *ffz*. (It is worth noting that *sf* does not appear in this repertoire.) It is likely that *ppp* suggests the use of the celeste stop (moderator) on Viennese pianos built before ca. 1840. Alongside Schubert calls at times explicitly for the use of the shifting soft pedal (*Mit Verschiebung*). For this reason it might be unwise to use the latter at every occurrence of *pp* on a Viennese piano, and this would be particularly inadvisable on today's pianos, which would make the especially delicate passages in *ppp* indistinguishable from those in *pp*.

Decrescendo and Diminuendo

Schubert distinguishes as a rule between *ritardando* (getting slower), *decrescendo* (getting softer), and *diminuendo* (getting softer *and* slower). Although this distinction has been challenged, it supported by several factors: Firstly, unlike Beethoven, who used *decrescendo* in his earlier music but shifted to *diminuendo* in later works, Schubert uses the two terms within single movements throughout his creative life. There can be no philological advantage to using two interchangeable terms when they mean the same thing. Secondly, one frequently encounters *a tempo* after *diminuendo*. One, however, never encounters *a tempo* after *decrescendo*. Thirdly, one can predict to a considerable degree when and where *diminuendo* will occur, namely at the end of exposition and recapitulation, at codas or at the retransition to the recapitulation.

Articulation

The clarity of articulation in which Viennese pianos excel is a central attribute of the Classical style. As pianos became more powerful and consequently increased in their sustaining power, slurs became longer and articulation markings less detailed. In the course of his creative life Beethoven increasingly used slurs and articulations to show not just the intended execution of his music, but its shape and direction. Schubert was, as most of his contemporaries, influenced by Beethoven's innovations in this regard; like Beethoven, he used the term *ligato* (not *legato*) with some frequency, whereas in the 18th century non-legato was the rule and legato the expressive effect, especially in keyboard writing. Nonetheless, Schubert's articulations still reflect to some degree the language of Mozart and Haydn. Thus, unarticulated notes are normally played with separation between them, the amount depending upon the expressive content.

According to Leopold Mozart's violin treatise[2] and other contemporaneous treatises, slurs not only prescribe legato playing, but are to be understood as decrescendos, with the last note normally lighter. This practice retained validity through the 19th century; eyewitnesses corroborate that Brahms inflected this way. As in Mozart and Haydn, when Alberti basses or related figures are slurred in keyboard music, the bottom note is meant to be sustained (known today as finger pedalling) throughout the group.

Execution of Dotted Rhythms

From the Baroque era until the early 20th century, it was common in passages using triplets for the long-short triplet rhythm (♩ ♪) to be notated with the dotted rhythm ♩. ♪, with the semiquaver (sixteenth note) executed together with the third triplet pulse. The exception to this convention was in slow tempi, where the notated semiquaver (sixteenth note) was played after the third triplet pulse[3] – a suggestion that could well apply to the *C minor Impromptu*, Op. 90/1, given its tempo designation of *Allegro molto moderato* – if the principal inference of the tempo indication lies with *molto moderato*. It bears mentioning, however, that in both the Schubert's autograph and in the first edition of the *Impromptu* the semiquaver (sixteenth note) of the ♩. ♪ rhythm is aligned with the third triplet pulse – if anything it is slightly before the third triplet pulse, never after. For this reason the present edition aligns the dotted rhythms with the triplets.

Ornaments

Well into the 19th century trills were executed from the upper neighboring tone and appoggiaturas were played on the beat. Chopin assumed upper note execution of his trills throughout his entire creative life. Nonetheless, exceptions to these conventions emerged in the 18th century and Schubert's lifetime was a time of transition. Main-note trills will be used primarily where they provide a more natural contour to the line, such as when preceded by a rapid scale passage up or down to the trill, where upper-note execution results either in a gap at the trill or a repeated tone. Schubert does not always write in the terminations of trills, even though these were conventionally assumed until at least the mid-19th century. Although there are occasional cases in which such terminations may be omitted, especially at faster tempi and for trills on short note values, these constitute the exception rather than the rule.

Pedalling

Schubert prescribes the use of sustaining pedal quite infrequently. It is likely, however, that Schubert reckoned with more frequent use of the damper-raising pedal.[4] In general, textures with slow harmonic rhythm in which few appoggiaturas or other stepwise melodic motion are present are well suited to the use of the sustaining pedal, whose potential use is not ruled out when, for example, the first note of a left-hand figure has a staccato dot or a stroke on it. On the other hand, the lighter, clearer sound of Viennese pianos of Schubert's time makes a more sparing use of pedal possible than is customary on today's instruments.

Remarks on the Individual Works

Impromptu Op. 90/1

The ornaments ♫ (cf. bar 19) and ⁕ (cf. bar 26, 181) are to be played before the beat; note that on-beat execution at bar 19 would produce parallel octaves with the bass while substituting a doubled dissonance (*c*) for the complete diminished seventh chord.

At bars 75–76 and parallel passages either pre-beat or on-beat execution is possible; the former seems more elegant; cf. bars 79–80, where the minim (half note) is explicitly on the beat.

At bar 107 the appoggiatura must be executed on the beat; otherwise parallel 5ths with the top voice would ensue.

Impromptu Op. 90/3

Bar 75, left hand, the appoggiatura could well indicate that the trill is to commence on the upper note (e♭♭).

Robert D. Levin

[1] I am grateful to Malcolm Bilson for his stimulating advice in the preparation of these notes.
[2] Leopold Mozart, *Versuch einer gründlichen Violinschule*, Augsburg, 1756, p. 135. English edition: *A Treatise on the Fundamental Principles of Violin Playing*, translated by Editha Knocker (Oxford[shire] and New York, 1948: Oxford University Press), p. 135.
[3] On this subject cf. Chapters II and III from Vol. IV of the 'Complete Theoretical and Practical Pianoforte School', Op. 500. English ed. published R. Cocks & Co., London, plate number 6797, p. 39, where Czerny refers to the 1st movement of Beethoven's 'Moonlight Sonata': 'The semiquaver must be struck after the last note of the triplet.' German edition: Carl Czerny, *Über den richtigen Vortrag der sämtlichen Beethoven'schen Klavierwerke*, in: *Vollständige theoretisch-practische Pianoforte-Schule op. 500*, vol. 4, chapter 2 and 3, ed. with a commentary by Paul Badura-Skoda, Vienna, 1970, p. 51.
[4] More generally, see David Rowland, *A History of Pianoforte Pedalling*, Cambridge, 1993.

PRÉFACE

Les *Quatre Impromptus* op. 90 de Franz Schubert constituent la première série de l'ensemble de huit *Impromptus* connus comme op. 90 et op. 142. Nous en ignorons la date exacte de composition, mais pour toutes sortes de raisons, on peut la situer au milieu de l'année 1827. Seuls les deux premiers numéros de l'opus 90 ont été édités du vivant du compositeur, chez Tobias Haslinger à Vienne. Leur publication a été annoncée dans le *Wiener Zeitung* du 10 décembre 1827 avec un numéro d'œuvre différent : 87. On ignore la raison pour laquelle les deux *Impromptus* op. 90/3 et op. 90/4 n'ont été publiés que longtemps après la mort de Schubert. C'est Tobias Haslinger lui-même (1787–1842) qui a agencé l'autographe pour la publication, mais ces pièces n'ont été éditées par les soins de son fils que 15 ans après la mort du père. Il semble que l'on ait considéré la transposition en sol majeur de la composition de sol bémol majeur et la subdivision de la mesure double (de 4/2 en 2/2) de l'op. 90/3 comme une facilité pour l'interprète. C'est sous cette forme que la composition s'est imposée jusque vers le milieu du XXᵉ siècle, bien qu'elle ait déjà été imprimée dans la tonalité originale dans l'ancienne Édition Schubert (1888). Mais du fait de cette subdivision, le flux naturel du morceau risque de se perdre et la transposition, si elle offre une facilité de lecture, n'apporte pas d'amélioration sur le plan de la difficulté technique, car dans la tonalité originale de sol bémol majeur, la pièce de Schubert est assez confortable pour la main.

On trouve divers exemples de ce titre autour des années 1820 et fait souvent référence aux six *Impromptus* op. 7 de Jan Václav Voríšek parus à Vienne chez Pietro Mechetti en 1822. Mais il existe également des Impromptus publiés par d'autres compositeurs renommés de l'époque, comme Johann Baptist Cramer, Carl Czerny, Heinrich Marschner, Ignaz Moscheles ou le jeune Franz Liszt. D'un point de vue historico-littéraire, le terme « Impromptu » est en fait un poème improvisé. On retrouve par exemple ce caractère d'improvisation dans diverses œuvres de Johann Baptist Cramer ou dans l'opus 3 de Franz Liszt, un *Impromptu brillant sur des Thèmes de Rossini et Spontini*. Par contre cette structure n'apparaît pas dans les *Impromptus* de Schubert, qui ont une architecture manifeste, à l'exception du premier morceau de l'op. 90, dont les variations se développent à partir d'un sujet de quatre mesures. On note d'ailleurs dans l'opus 90 la dominance de pièces nettement architectoniques en forme tripartite, se terminant souvent par une coda.

L'autographe de l'opus 90 de Schubert nous est parvenu et il existe en outre une première ébauche autographe de l'*Impromptu* op. 90/1. C'est l'autographe qui sert de source principale à la présente nouvelle édition, les premières éditions constituant des sources secondaires. Il n'existe que peu de copies manuscrites contemporaines des *Impromptus* op. 90. Parmi les manuscrits les plus importantes se trouvent les copies de la célèbre Collection Witteczek-Spaun, conservés depuis 1865 dans les Archives de la Société des Amis de la Musique *(Archiv der Gesellschaft der Musikfreunde)* à Vienne. Les copies de cette collection sont fidèles aux autographes mais comportent ici et là des indications d'articulation qui suivent judicieusement les principes établis par le compositeur et ne peuvent dès lors être ignorés.

L'autographe de Schubert est facilement lisible. La hauteur des notes et les valeurs rythmiques sont nettement reconnaissables. Mais il est parfois négligent dans l'annotation des altérations. Il note généralement les indications de dynamique avant la note concernée, ce qui entraîne parfois des erreurs dans les premières éditions. Les signes d'articulation sont souvent placés entre les portées, et il n'est pas évident de savoir s'ils concernent vraiment les deux portées. La position des signes de liaison pose parfois problème en étant imprécise. L'articulation est rarement peaufinée. Lorsqu'il a choisi un modèle d'articulation, Schubert ne le note que rarement en détail. Les signes d'articulation peuvent être indiqués négligemment ou manquer totalement, sous-entendant un *simile*. La comparaison avec des passages parallèles ne mène à rien parce qu'ils peuvent diverger dans le détail et qu'il n'est pas évident de savoir si Schubert a procédé délibérément à ces modifications ou si elles sont intervenues par hasard.

Soulignons encore deux particularités dans l'écriture de Schubert : l'utilisation des signes d'accentuation et la variabilité dans la notation des points et traits d'articulation. L'abondance des signes d'accentuation donne aux autographes de Schubert une apparence caractéristique. Il est parfois difficile de différencier les accents étirés en largeur des signes de *decrescendo*. Dans la présente nouvelle édition, nous avons accordé la préférence aux signes d'accentuation, dans la mesure où ils ne sont pas situés dans le contexte direct d'un *decrescendo*. Lorsque Schubert n'écrit pas à la va-vite, on remarque qu'il fait une différenciation nette entre les points et les traits d'articulation. Le choix s'opère en premier lieu en fonction du contexte dynamique : dans les passages *piano*, Schubert utilise presque exclusivement des points, et dans les passages *forte* plutôt des traits. Dans les passages *portato*, on constate que les points s'adaptent de manière suggestive au tempo. Dans l'autographe de l'*Impromptu* en sol bémol majeur op. 90/3, les points de *portato* sont de ce fait très larges et se rapprochent presque de traits de *tenuto* ; mais ni les copies manuscrites contemporaines ni la première édition ne tiennent compte de cette différence.

Dans la présente édition, nous avons utilisé l'autographe de Schubert comme source principale. Les ajouts faits à partir des sources secondaires sont par principe indiqués entre parenthèses. Par ailleurs, nous avons souligné, dans des annotations, les additions faites à partir des sources secondaires manuscrites. Les ajouts de l'éditeur sont mis en évidence entre crochets.

Ulrich Leisinger
(Traduction Geneviève Geffray)

NOTES SUR L'INTERPRÉTATION[1]

Exécution et expression

Dans tous les aspects de la pratique d'interprétation, il est indispensable de faire la différence entre l'exécution – suivant les règles générales d'interprétations de l'époque indépendamment des particularités spécifiques du passage concerné – et l'expression, qui est en relation directe avec le caractère exprimé par un passage donné. Tous les détails traités par la suite doivent être considérés dans ce contexte. Ainsi l'exécution des ♩♪ notées toujours dans le même rythme dans l'*Impromptu* en ut mineur op. 90/1 pourrait varier par la suite selon les divers caractères :

Mes. 1 et suiv. : réalisation rythmique relativement exacte à l'intérieur du *legato* ;
Mes. 5 et suiv. : réalisation légèrement surpointée avec une double croche jouée un peu plus tard et plus courte que dans la réalisation stricte de sa valeur, conformément au rythme de marche du passage ;
Mes. 41 et suiv. : adapté au rythme des triolets conformément à la mélodie *cantabile* très expressive (cf. infra les conseils d'exécution des rythmes pointés).

Dynamique

Schubert prescrit une répartition dynamique allant de *fff* à *ppp* ainsi que les symboles de *sforzato fp*, *fz* et *ffz*. Pour les pianos viennois construits avant 1840, *ppp* signifie l'emploi de la céleste. En outre, Schubert exige parfois la pédale *una corda* (*Mit Verschiebung* – « Avec sourdine »). Pour cette raison, il semble peu recommandé d'y avoir recours chaque fois que l'on rencontre l'injonction *pp* ; nous le déconseillons même fortement sur les pianos modernes, car dans ce cas, on ne pourrait guère faire la différence entre les passages spécialement délicats indiqués *ppp* et ceux marqués *pp*.

Decrescendo et diminuendo

Schubert fait généralement la distinction entre *ritardando* (devenant plus lent), *decrescendo* (devenant plus doux) et *diminuendo* (devenant plus doux *et* plus lent). Cette différenciation a certes été mise en doute à diverses occasions, mais elle est étayée par une série d'observations : Premièrement : Contrairement à Beethoven, qui utilisa *decrescendo* dans ses œuvres plus anciennes mais choisit plus tard le terme *diminuendo*, Schubert a eu recours parallèlement aux deux formes tout au long de sa vie, à l'intérieur d'un même mouvement. Il ne semble pas y avoir d'avantage philologique à utiliser deux notions interchangeables si elles ont la même signification. Deuxièmement : On rencontre souvent *a tempo* après *diminuendo*. On ne rencontre par contre jamais *a tempo* après *decrescendo*. Troisièmement : On peut prévoir avec forte probabilité quand et où on rencontrera *diminuendo* – à savoir : à la fin de l'exposition et de la reprise, dans la coda ou dans le pont qui conduit à la reprise.

Articulation

La clarté d'articulation qui caractérise les pianos viennois est l'un des attributs essentiels du style classique. Lorsque les pianos gagnèrent en volume et parvinrent à résonner plus longuement, les signes de tenue se rallongèrent et les indications d'articulation furent moins détaillées. Au cours de sa vie, Beethoven utilisa toujours plus de signes de tenue et d'articulations pour souligner non seulement la manière dont il voulait qu'on interprète sa musique, mais aussi sa forme et sa direction. Comme la plupart de ses contemporains, Schubert subit l'influence des innovations de Beethoven en ce domaine ; comme Beethoven il utilise souvent la notion *ligato* (pas *legato*), alors qu'au XVIIIe siècle le *non-legato* était de règle et que le *legato* était utilisé pour obtenir un certain effet expressif. Mais les indications d'articulation de Schubert reflètent encore jusqu'à un certain point le langage musical de Mozart et Haydn. Ainsi, les sons dépourvus de signes d'articulation sont-ils généralement détachés les uns des autres, le degré du détaché dépendant du contenu expressif.

D'après l'*École du violon* de Leopold Mozart et d'autres traités contemporains, les signes de liaison n'indiquent pas seulement un jeu *legato*, mais peuvent être interprétés comme un *decrescendo*, la dernière note devant normalement être jouée plus légèrement.[2] Cette pratique s'est maintenue tout au long du XIXe siècle ; des témoins contemporains ont confirmé que Brahms utilisait encore cette technique. Tout comme chez Mozart et Haydn, le son de basse était soutenu sur tout le groupe (pédale de doigt) lorsqu'on rencontrait des signes de liaison dans les basses d'Alberti ou dans des figures similaires de la musique pour piano.

Exécution des rythmes pointés

De l'époque baroque au début du XXe siècle, il était usuel, dans les passages avec triolets, de noter avec un rythme pointé ♪. les triolets long-court ♩ ♪, la double croche étant attaquée en même temps que le troisième battement du triolet. La seule exception à cette convention était faite dans le tempo lent, où la double croche était jouée après le troisième battement du triolet.[3] Du fait de l'indication de tempo *Allegro molto moderato*, ceci pourrait s'appliquer également à l'*Impromptu* en ut mineur op. 90/1, si l'on met l'accent sur *molto moderato*. Mais il convient de noter que non seulement dans le manuscrit autographe, mais encore dans la première édition, la double croche tombe, dans un rythme ♪., en même temps que le troisième battement du triolet – donc, si tant est, la double croche peut tomber un tout petit peu avant le battement du triolet, mais jamais après. C'est la raison pour laquelle dans la présente édition, nous avons harmonisé les rythmes pointés et les triolets.

Ornements

Jusqu'à une date avancée du XIXe siècle, les trilles étaient attaqués par la note secondaire supérieure et l'appogiature était jouée sur le temps. Chopin eut recours aux trilles « par en haut » tout au long de sa vie. Mais au XVIIIe siècle, on rencontre des exceptions à cette règle, et l'époque de Schubert est une période de transition. Les trilles à partir de la note principale sont utilisés principalement s'ils entraînent un cours naturel de la mélodie, par exemple s'ils sont précédés par un passage ascendant ou descendant rapide. Schubert n'impose pas toujours une terminaison aux trilles, bien que ceux-ci aient fait partie de la norme au moins jusqu'au milieu du XIXe siècle. Il existe certes des cas où l'on peut omettre ces terminaisons, en particulier dans un tempo rapide et dans des trilles sur des notes courtes ; mais c'est plus l'exception que la règle.

Emploi de la pédale

Schubert ne prescrit explicitement l'emploi de la pédale (droite) que très rarement. Mais il semble évident que Schubert comptait sur l'emploi plus fréquent de la pédale pour activer l'étouffoir.[4] En règle générale, les sections au rythme harmonique lent, dans lesquelles on ne rencontre que peu d'appogiatures ou autres mouvements mélodiques par degrés de secondes, semblent bien se prêter à l'usage de la pédale de soutien. On ne peut pas non plus exclure l'emploi de la pédale si, par exemple, la première note d'une figure de la main gauche a un point de staccato ou un trait d'articulation. Par ailleurs la sonorité plus limpide et plus claire des pianos viennois autorise un emploi de la pédale plus parcimonieux que sur les instruments modernes.

Remarques concernant les œuvres individuelles

Impromptu op. 90/1

Les ornements ♫ (mes. 19) et ∾ (mes. 26 et 181) doivent être joués avant le temps ; il faut noter que si l'on joue sur le temps à la mes. 19, cela entraînerait des mouvements parallèles d'octaves avec la basse et conduirait en même temps au doublement de la dissonance (*ut*) à la place de l'accord de septième diminué.

Aux mes. 75–76 et dans les passages parallèles, il est possible de jouer avant ou sur le temps ; cette dernière solution semble plus élégante. Cf. mes. 79–80 où la blanche est située explicitement sur le temps.

À la mes. 107, l'appogiature doit être jouée sur le temps pour éviter les quintes parallèles avec la partie supérieure.

Impromptu op. 90/3

À la mes. 75, l'appogiature à la main gauche semble indiquer que le trille doit être attaqué par la note supérieure (*mi* ♭).

Robert D. Levin
(Traduction Geneviève Geffray)

---

[1] Je remercie Malcolm Bilson pour les suggestions et les conseils qu'il m'a prodigués lorsque je travaillais à ces Conseils d'interprétation.

[2] Leopold Mozart, *Versuch einer gründlichen Violinschule*, Augsbourg 1756, p. 135.

[3] Voir à ce sujet l'indication de Carl Czerny dans *Über den richtigen Vortrag der sämtlichen Beethoven'schen Klavierwerke* (dans : *Vollständige theoretisch-practische Pianoforte-Schule op. 500*, vol. 4, chapitre 2 et 3, éd. et annoté de Paul Badura-Skoda, Vienne 1970, p. 51), où selon lui, dans le premier mouvement de la *Sonate au Clair de lune*, la ♪ ne doit *pas* être jouée en même temps que le troisième battement du triolet.

[4] Cf. sur ce sujet général David Rowland, *A History of Pianoforte Pedalling*, Cambridge 1993.

Vier Impromptus
op. 90 / D 899

Franz Schubert
(1797–1828)

*) Rhythmische Notation nach dem Autograph / Rhythmical notation according to the autograph / Notation du rythme selon l'autographe

*) Besser / better / meilleur:

Franz Schubert, *Impromptu in c-Moll op. 90/1* (D 899/1)
Autographer Bleistiftentwurf, fol. 1r

Franz Schubert, *Impromptu in C minor Op. 90/1* (D 899/1)
Autograph draft written in pencil, fol. 1r

Franz Schubert, *Impromptu en ut mineur op. 90/1* (D 899/1)
Première ébauche écrite au crayon, fol. 1r

Wien, Wienbibliothek im Rathaus, Musiksammlung, MH 145

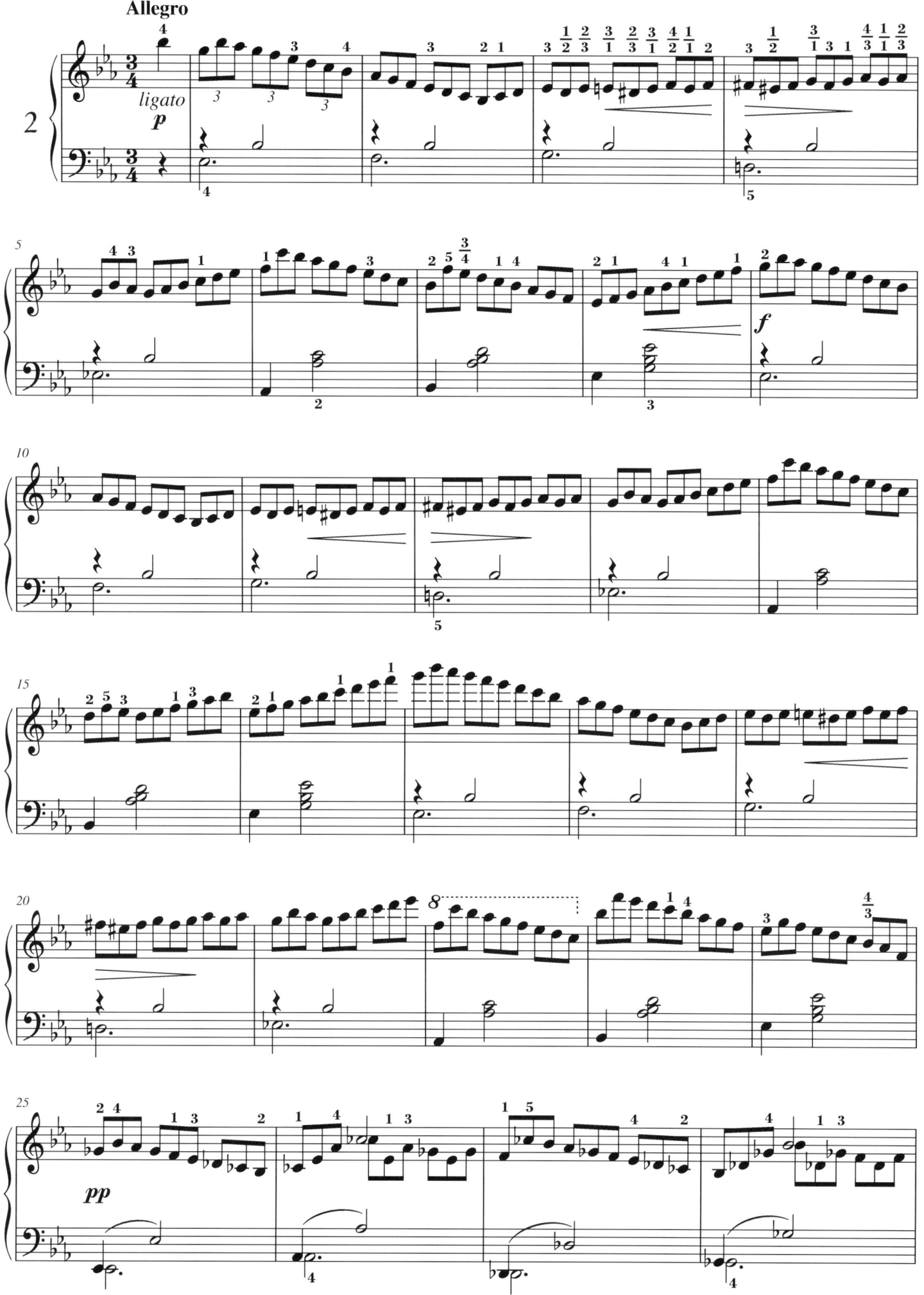

*) Siehe Einzelanmerkungen / See Detailed Notes / Voir Notes Détaillées

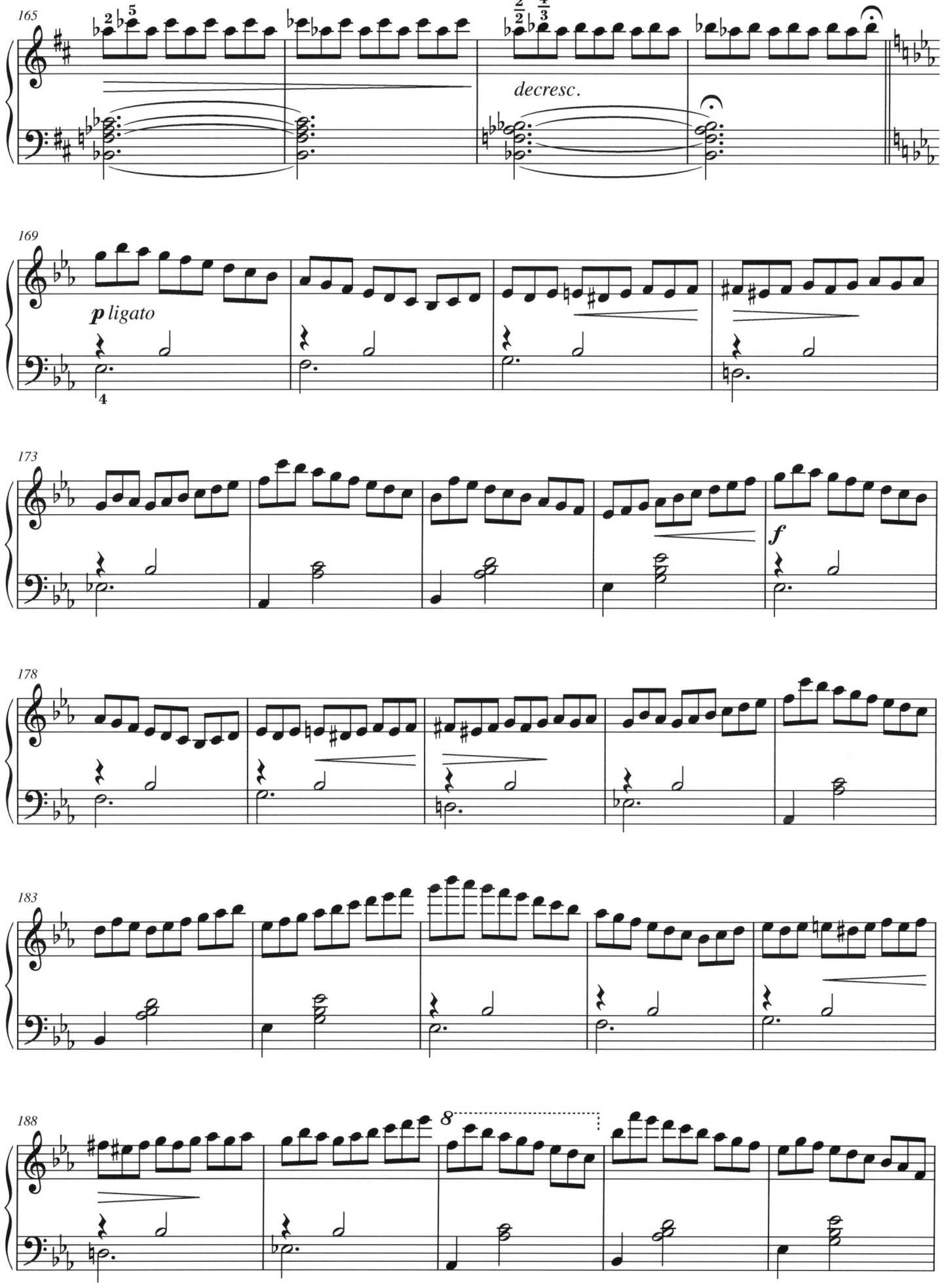

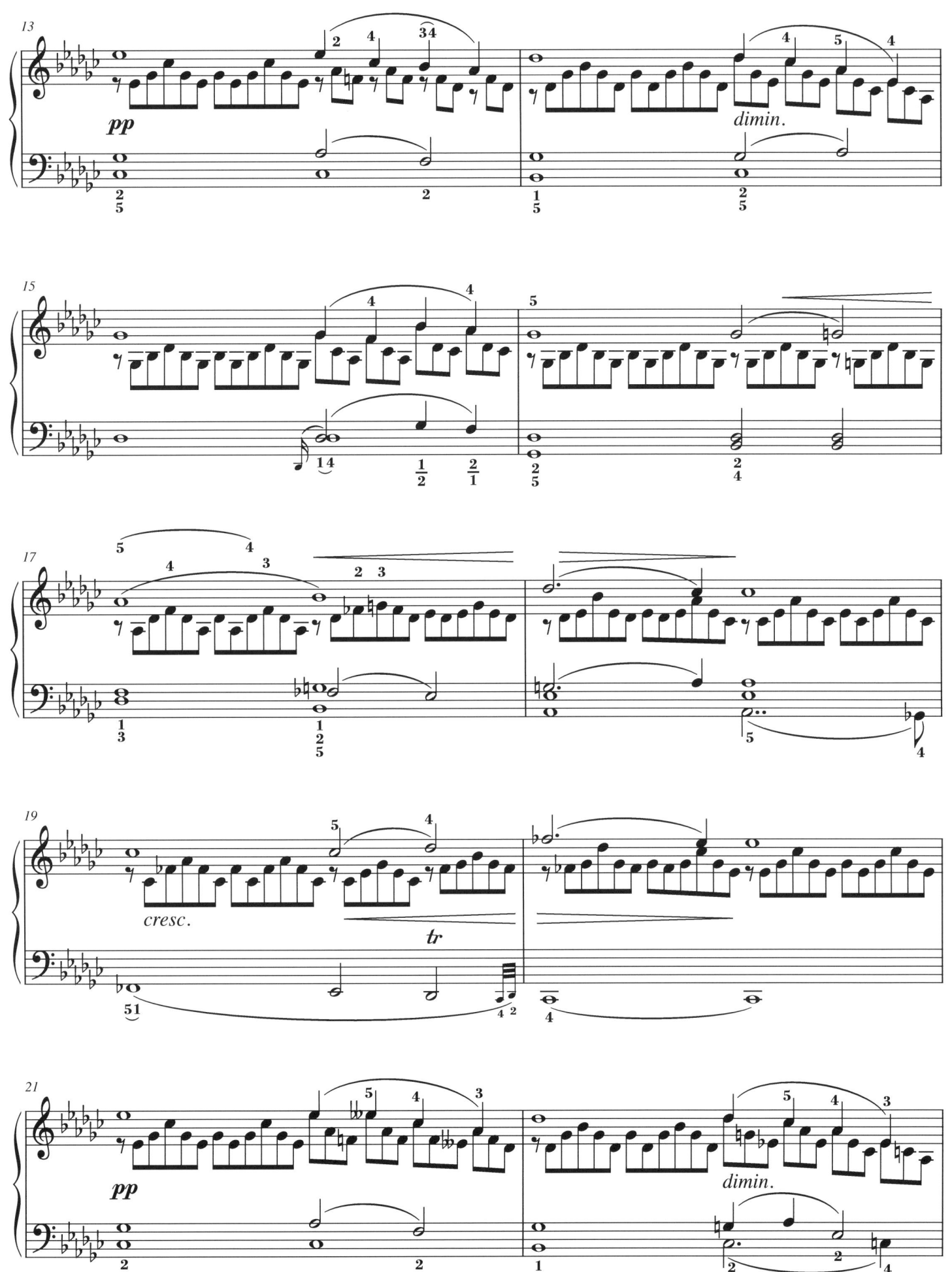

*) *fz* in T. 28 und 29 nur in Abschrift Hölbing / *fz* in b. 28 and 29 in manuscript copy Hölbing only / *fz* dans mes. 28 et 29 seulement dans la copie en manuscrit Hölbing

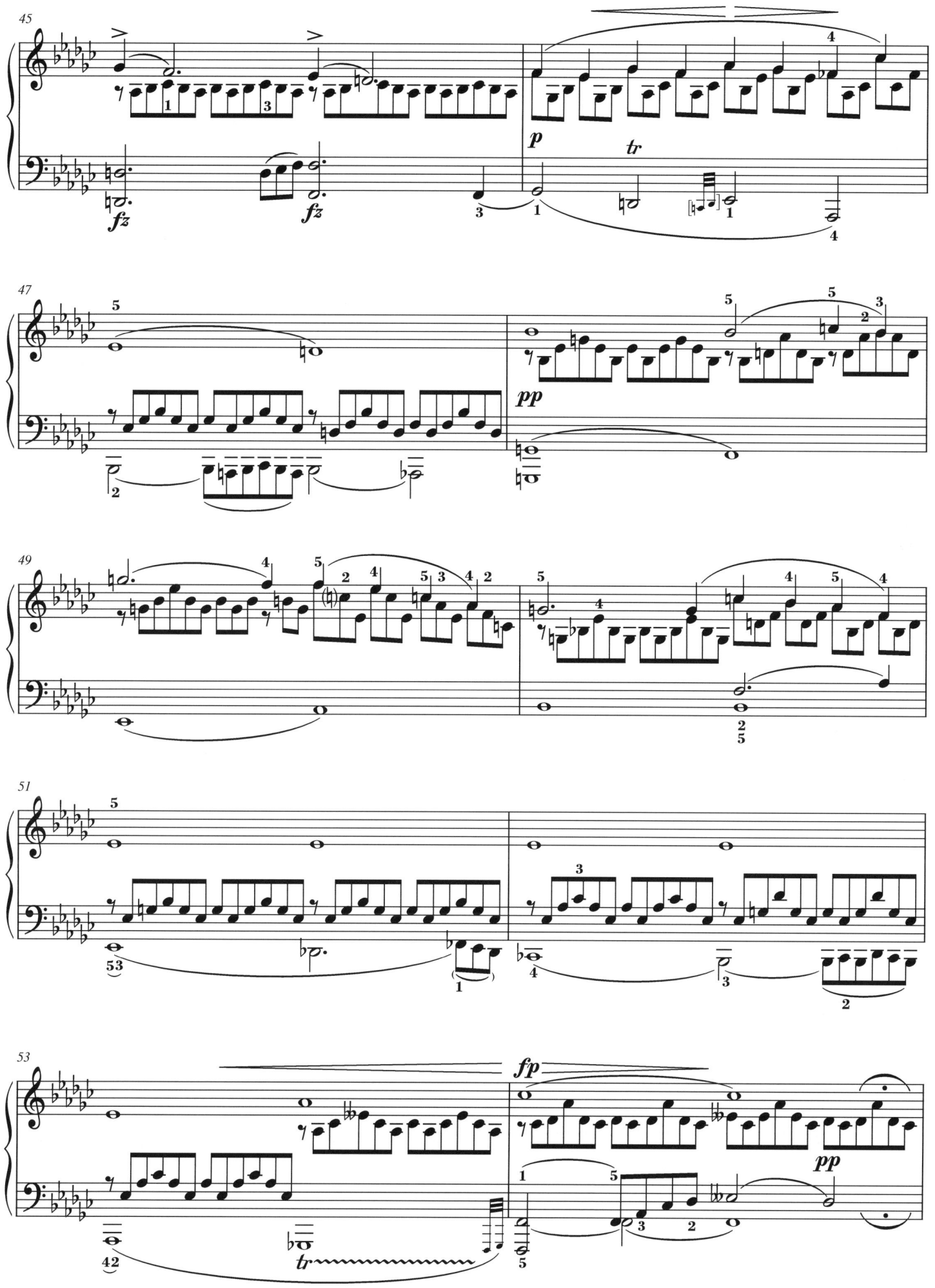

Franz Schubert, *Impromptu in Ges-Dur op. 90/3* (D 899/3)
Erstausgabe, Beginn der nach G-Dur transponierten Fassung
Mit abweichender Lesart zu Beginn der 4. Akkolade

Franz Schubert, *Impromptu in G flat major Op. 90/3* (D 899/3)
First Edition, beginning of the version transposed to G major
With a divergent reading at the beginning of the 4th system

Franz Schubert, *Impromptu en sol bémol majeur op. 90/3* (D 899/3)
Première Édition, début de la version transposée en sol majeur
Avec une lecture divergente au début de la 4e portée

Deutscher Privatbesitz

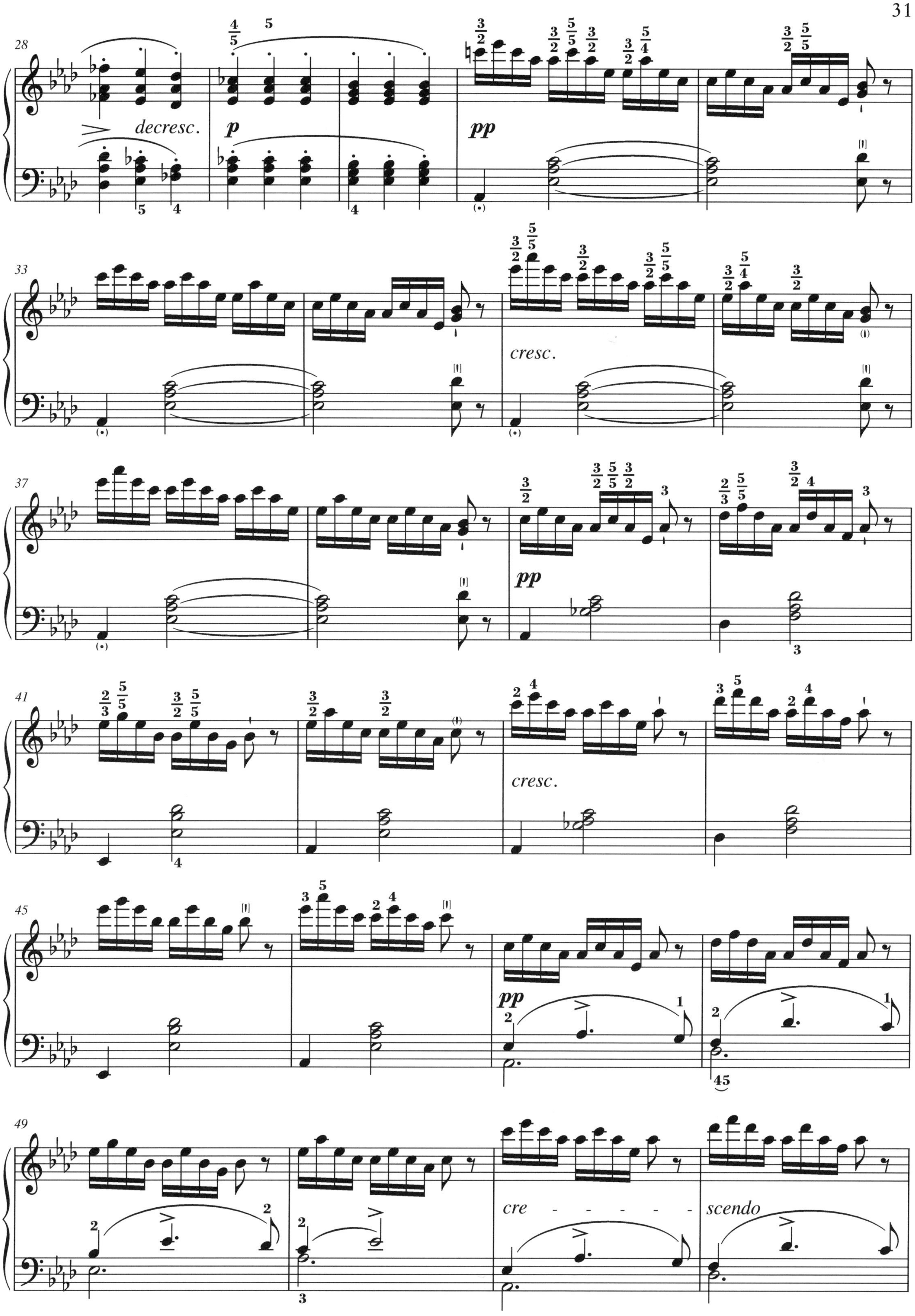
decresc.
p
pp
cresc.
pp
cresc.
pp
cre - - - - - - scendo

KRITISCHE ANMERKUNGEN

Abkürzungen

0	Auftakt
a.c.	ante correcturam (vor Korrektur)
Bg(n).	Bogen (Bögen)
Bl(l).	Blatt (Blätter)
erg.	ergänzt
fol.	folio
gem.	gemäß
Hbg(n).	Haltebogen (-bögen)
hs.	handschriftlich
korr.	korrigiert
l.N.	letzte Note
NA	vorliegende Neuausgabe
OS	Oberstimme
o.S.	oberes System
p.c.	post correcturam (nach Korrektur)
PN	Plattennummer
Pst(n).	Parallelstelle(n)
r	recto
S.	Seite
T.	Takt
US	Unterstimme
u.S.	unteres System
v	verso
vgl.	vergleiche
vl.N.	vorletzte Note
vs.	versehentlich
Zz.	Zählzeit
→	angeglichen an

Quellen

A Autographe Reinschrift von op. 90/1–4. 12 querformatige Blätter (16 x 24 cm) mit 23 beschriebenen Seiten. Kein Werktitel, nur nicht autographer Namenszug *Fr: Schubert.* in der rechten oberen Ecke der 1. Seite. Von Schubert stammt die Instrumentenangabe *Pianoforte* (wiederholt auf fol. 4r) und die Zählung *№ I.* auf fol. 1r, während die Angaben *Impromptu., № 1. in C. moll.* und die Verlagsnummer *(5071.)* auf fol. 1r (bzw. *(5072.)* auf fol. 4r) von der Hand Tobias Haslingers hinzugefügt wurden. Zu op. 90/3 ist von der Hand Tobias Haslingers angegeben: *Im ganzen Takt und in G-Dur um zu schreiben*; entsprechend sind zusätzliche Taktstriche in der Taktmitte (nur in T. 1–4) gezogen.
New York, Pierpont Morgan Library, Music Manuscripts and Printed Music, S384.I34.

Ae Autographer Entwurf. 8 querformatige, mit Bleistift beschriebene Blätter (16 x 24,7 cm) mit 11 beschriebenen Seiten. Ohne Werktitel, Tempobezeichnung oder Autorenangabe. Der Entwurf ist vollständig und umfasst 183 Takte; diese entsprechen weitgehend der endgültigen Fassung (unter Auslassung der Takte 18–33, 180–183 und 192)[1].
Wien, Wienbibliothek im Rathaus, Musiksammlung, MH 145.

EA1 Erstausgabe von op. 90/1–2 (als *op. 87*) in zwei Heften bei Tobias Haslinger (Wien 1827). Titel: *№* [hs.: *1.* bzw. *2.*] / *Impromptu* / *pour le* / *PIANO = FORTE* / *PAR* / *Franz Schubert.* / *OEUVRE 87.* / *Propriété de l'Editeur* / *Vienne, chez Tobie Haslinger,* / *Editeur de Musique* / *dans la maison de la Caisse d'Epargne,* / *sur le Graben № 572.* / [sehr blass!] *Jos. List. sc.* //. Kopftitel: *IMPROMPTU.*
Heft 1: PN: T. H. 5071.; Preis: f. 45x C.M./12 gr.
Heft 2: PN: T. H. 5072.; Preis: f. 45x C.M./12 gr.
Exemplare: Wien, Österreichische Nationalbibliothek, Musiksammlung, S.H. Schubert 326 (op. 90/1) und L 18 Kaldeck M.S. 41118-4°/2 (op. 90/2).

EA2 Erstausgabe von op. 90/3–4 in zwei (als 3 und 4 gezählten) Heften[2] bei Karl Haslinger (Wien, 1857). Titel: *No.* [Stempel: *3* bzw. *4*] / *Impromptu* / *pour le* / *PIANO = FORTE* / *PAR* / *Franç. Schubert.* / *OEUVRE 90.* / *Propriété de l'Editeur* / *Vienne, chez Charles Haslinger q^m Tobie,* / *Marchand de Musique etc. de la Cour Imp. et Royale.* //.
Heft 3: Verlagsverzeichnis *NEUESTE PIANO-FORTE-MUSIK.* PN: (12.075.); Preis: 45x C.M.
Heft 4: PN: (12.076.); Preis: 45x C.M.
In Übereinstimmung mit den Einträgen Haslingers in **A** ist op. 90/3 in **EA2** im einfachen ¢-Takt (2/2) notiert und nach G-Dur transponiert. Die postume Erstausgabe ist damit für dieses Stück als Referenzquelle nur eingeschränkt brauchbar.
Exemplare: Wien, Österreichische Nationalbibliothek, Musiksammlung, S.H. Schubert 334 (Heft 3); und S.H. Schubert 335 (Heft 4)[3].

TA Titelauflage der Erstausgabe von op. 90/1–2 in 2 Heften bei Tobias Haslinger (Wien, kurz nach 1827). Titel: *№.* [hs.: *1* bzw. *2*] / *Impromptu / pour le / PIANO = FORTE / PAR / Franç. Schubert. / OEUVRE 90. / Propriété de l'Editeur / Vienne, chez Tobie Haslinger, / Edi-

---

[1] Der Entwurf ist wiedergegeben in *Franz Schubert: Impromptus, Moments musicaux, Drei Klavierstücke. Nach Autographen und Erstdrucken herausgegeben und mit Fingersätzen versehen von Paul Badura-Skoda*, Wien: Universal Edition, 1969, seit 1973 Wiener Urtext Edition, UT 50001, Anhang, S. XXII–XXIX.

[2] Die Impromptus op. 90/1–2 wurden (mit beibehaltener Plattennummer und Seiteneinteilung) damals neu gestochen; diese Ausgabe (Exemplare in der Österreichischen Nationalbibliothek, Wien, Musiksammlung, S.H. Schubert 328 bzw. S.H. Schubert 332) bleibt im Folgenden unberücksichtigt.

[3] Da die Exemplare in der Österreichischen Nationalbibliothek, S.H. Schubert 333 und S.H. Schubert 334, offenbar als Stichvorlage für eine nicht identifizierte spätere Ausgabe dienten, wurde zusätzlich jeweils ein Exemplar aus deutschem Privatbesitz herangezogen. Dieses Exemplar weist zusätzlich die Verlagsangabe *Leipsic, chez B. Hermann.* auf.

teur de Musique / dans la maison de la Caisse d'Epargne, / sur le Graben № 572. //. Kopftitel: *IMPROMPTU.*
Heft 1: PN: T. H. 5071.; Preis: f. 45x C.M./12 gr.
Heft 2: PN: T. H. 5072.; Preis: f. 45x C.M./12 gr.
Exemplare: Deutscher Privatbesitz und Wien, Österreichische Nationalbibliothek, Musiksammlung, S.H. Schubert 327 (op. 90/1) und S.H. Schubert 331 (op. 90/2).

AbN Abschrift Noraberg. Abschrift von op. 90/1 (wohl Kopie nach **EA1**) aus der 1. Hälfte des 19. Jahrhunderts. 6 hochformatige Blätter mit 12 beschriebenen Seiten. Titelseite: *Impromptu / pour le / Piano-Forte / par / Franz Schubert. //.*
Privatbesitz, letzter bekannter Besitzer: Lilly Noraberg, Graz.

AbH Abschrift Hölbing. Abschrift von op. 90/3 nach dem Autograph im Album der Familie Hölbing, S. 73–77, datiert: *Wien am 26. September 1854.* Mit zahlreichen Eintragungen des 19. und 20. Jahrhunderts. Titel: *Impromtu* [sic] *von Fr. Schubert.* Zueignung auf S. 77: *Mögen Sie sich zuweilen freundlich erinnern / Ihres aufrichtig ergebenen / Gahy* (wohl Josef von Gahy, 1793–1864), darunter Eintragungen von Elly Ney (datiert 10. Dezember 1959 und 29. September 1961) sowie von Friedrich Wührer (19. November 1972)[4].
Privatbesitz Familie Hölbing, derzeit Leihgabe in der Schubert-Gedenkstätte Atzenbrugg.

AbW Abschrift Witteczek-Spaun. Abschrift von op. 90/3 und op. 90/4 durch Weiser (Vorname nicht bekannt), den Hauptkopisten der Sammlung Witteczek-Spaun. 10 hochformatige Blätter mit 19 beschriebenen Seiten. Autorenangabe: *F: Schubert* auf fol. 39r.
Wien, Gesellschaft der Musikfreunde, Archiv und Bibliothek, Witteczek-Spaun, Bd. 60a, fol. 39r–48v.

Die nachstehenden Einzelanmerkungen folgen dem Schema: Takt – System/Stimme – Zeichen im Takt (Note, Akkord oder Pause) bzw. Zählzeit – Bemerkung.

Impromptu in c-Moll op. 90/1 (D 899/1)

Hauptquelle: **A**, Referenzquelle: **EA**

Einzelanmerkungen

In **EA** sind zahlreiche Bögen kürzer als in **A**; statt Staccato-Punkten werden dort durchweg Artikulations-Striche gesetzt; in **A** als einzelne kleine Sechzehntel notierte Vorschlagsnoten werden in **EA** als kleine durchstrichene Achtel wiedergegeben. In **A** und **EA** ist eine recht konsistente Angleichung von Punktierungen und Triolen vorgenommen (siehe auch *Hinweise zur Interpretation*).

Takt	System	Zeichen	Bemerkung
1f., 9f., 17f., 95f., 103f.	o.S.	Zz. 4	**EA**: Bg. nur bis T. 1, 9, 17, 95 bzw. 103, l.N.
12–13	o.S.		**A**: Bg. vor Zeilenwechsel nur bis T. 12, l.N.; NA folgt **EA**
19	o.S.	1	**EA**: Vorschlagsnoten: ♪ statt ♫
60			**EA**: *mf* bereits zu o.S., 2. Note
64	u.S.	1–3	**A**, **EA**: Bg. 1.–4. Note
65			**EA**: *f* erst auf Zz. 4
73	o.S.		**A**: Bg. beginnt zwischen 1. und 2. Note, **EA**: Bg. nur zu 3.–6. Note; NA → Pstn. T. 52 und 71
75, 76	o.S.		**A**: Bg. beginnt zwischen 1. und 2. Note; NA folgt **EA** (vgl. auch T. 74 und 79ff.)
77	o.S.		**EA**: 2. Bg. nur vl.N. – l.N.
77			**A**: > nur 1.–2. Note (weit vor 1. Note beginnend); NA folgt **EA**
81	o.S. OS	5–7	**EA**: Bg. nur vl.N. – l.N.
97, 98	o.S.		**A**: taktweise mit Bg.; NA folgt **EA**
104	o.S. OS	3–5	**EA**: Bg. nur vl.N. – l.N.
125	o.S.	1	**A**: Notenkopf tief angesetzt, auch als *c″* zu lesen
135	o.S.	1	**A**: Faser im Notenpapier, kein Staccato-Punkt
154	o.S.		**A**: Bg. beginnt zwischen 1. und 2. Note; NA → Pst. T. 152f. und **EA** (vgl. auch die Bemerkung zu T. 75, 76)
161	u.S.		**A**: Portato nur 1.–2. Note und nachfolgender Bg. 3.–5. Note; NA → Pst. T. 88 und **EA**

Impromptu in Es-Dur op. 90/2 (D 899/2)

Hauptquelle: **A**, Referenzquelle: **EA**

Einzelanmerkungen

In **A** sind die Takte 166 bzw. 168 ursprünglich nicht notiert (nachträglich mit Wiederholungszeichen und Vermerk *bis* eingefügt), in NA Realisierung gemäß **EA** p.c. (dort Plattenkorrektur). In **A** sind die Takte 169–250 als Wiederholung von T. 1–82 nicht ausgeschrieben, sondern ihre Wiederholung nur durch den Hinweis *D.C. al Segno* angezeigt, entsprechend steht nach T. 82 mit Blick auf T. 251: *Hier folgt beym 2ten Mahl das Coda.* Die Schlusstakte (T. 277–283) wurden ursprünglich auf fol. 11r notiert, dann dort ausgestrichen und auf fol. 7r nahezu gleichlautend wiederholt (nachdem zwei zusätzliche Doppelblätter in die Handschrift eingelegt worden waren).

Takt	System	Zz.	Bemerkung
0	o.S.		**EA**: *legato* statt *ligato*
77 (245)	u.S.	Zz. 1	**EA**: ♪ 𝄾 analog T. 78f. (= Lesart von **A** a.c.?, dort

---
[4] Das Album enthält zudem auf Schubert bezogene Einträge von D 547 (S. 32; Emma Spaun), D 823 (S. 38; Hedwig Hardtmuth) und D 915 (S. 71–72; Spaun).

			wohl durch Rasur zu ↑ korrigiert)
86	u.S.	2	**EA**: mit > (vgl. aber T. 94)
90, 92	o.S. US	Zz. 3	**A, EA** (hier auch T. 91): ♪ 𝄾; NA gleicht an das vorherrschende Muster (↑) an.
111	u.S.	1	**A**: Faser im Notenpapier, kein Staccato-Punkt
123			**EA**: ohne *p*
168	o.S.	l.N.	**EA**: ohne ⌢
184–185			**EA**: mit *cresc.* in T. 184 und *f* T. 185, 1. Note; vgl. aber T. 16–17
251			**EA**: ohne Bezeichnung *Coda*
279	u.S.	1	**A**: die erste Niederschrift auf fol. 11r ohne *es*

Impromptu in Ges-Dur op. 90/3 (D 899/3)

Hauptquelle: **A**, Referenzquellen: **AbH, AbW**

Einzelanmerkungen

EA weist zahlreiche zusätzliche dynamische Angaben auf: T. 4, Zz. 3: *p*; T. 6, Zz. 3+: *cresc.*; T. 8, Zz. 1: *p*; T. 31, Zz. 1: ⎯; T. 31, Zz. 2: ⎯; T. 31, Zz. 3: *decresc.*; T. 32, Zz. 1: *pp* (statt in T. 31); T. 47, Zz. 3: *decresc.*; T. 52, Zz. 3: *cresc.*; T. 57, Zz. 2: *cresc.*; T. 58, Zz. 3: *p*; T. 60, Zz. 4: *cresc.*; T. 62, Zz. 1: *p*

5, 59	u.S.	Zz. 4	**EA**: [musical notation]
11	o./u.S.	1	**A**: ♭ vor *fes* bzw. *fes'* fehlt; erg. gem. **AbW** (in **EA** analog vorhanden)
31		Zz. 1	**EA**: ohne *pp*
54	u.S.		**A, AbW, AbH**: vs. in halb so großen Notenwerten notiert
74	o.S.		**EA**: ⎯ erst ab T. 76
79ff.			**EA**: ohne Wechsel der Generalvorzeichnung

Impromptu in As-Dur op. 90/4 (D 899/4)

Hauptquelle: **A**, Referenzquellen: **EA, AbW**

Einzelanmerkungen

In **A** sind die Takte 55–56 nicht notiert, als Wiederholung der Takte 53–54 sind sie mittels *bis*-Vermerk angegeben; die Takte 42 und 66 sind nachträglich eingefügt. Die Takte 171–273 sind als Wiederholung von T. 1–102 in **A** nicht ausgeschrieben, ihre Wiederholung nur durch *D.C.* angezeigt; auf fol. 11r waren ursprünglich die letzten 7 Takte von op. 90/2 notiert (vgl. fol. 7r).

11–12	u.S. US	2ff.	**AbW**: vs. jeweils *es* statt *ges*
23	o./u.S.		**A, AbW, EA**: Bg. bereits ab 1. Note, in **EA** 1. Note zusätzlich mit Portato-Punkt
25, 27	u.S.		**AbW**: Portato bereits ab 1. Note; **EA**: T. 25, 1. Note mit Staccato-Punkt
29	o.S.		**A, AbW**: Portato-Bg. erst ab 2. Note; NA → u.S. und **EA**
51, 88	u.S. OS	2	**AbW**: vs. ohne Augmentationspunkt
74–75	o.S.		**AbW**: ein Bg. über die Zweitaktgruppe
78, 79	o.S.		**AbW**: Bg. jeweils über den ganzen Takt
107			**EA**: ohne Angabe *Trio*
116, 118	o.S. OS	2ff.	**EA**: jede Note mit >
116, 118	u.S. US	2ff.	**EA**: jede ↑ mit >
129	u.S.	2	**EA**: *Gis/His/dis* statt *Gis*
149	u.S.	1	**AbW**: *Kontra-H* mit zusätzlichem Viertelhals nach unten
151	u.S.	1	**EA**: *D* mit zusätzlichem Viertelhals nach unten
152	u.S.	3, 5	**AbW**: ohne zusätzlichen Viertelhals nach unten
153	u.S.	3	**AbW, EA**: *Kontra-A* mit zusätzlichem Viertelhals nach unten
209–213	u.S.	1	**EA**: jeweils mit Staccato-Punkt (nicht aber an Pst. T. 39–43)
217–233, 250–268	o.S.	9	**EA**: jeweils mit Staccato-Punkt
268			**EA**: *ffz* statt *ff*

CRITICAL NOTES

Abbreviations

0	up-beat
a.c.	ante correcturam (before correction)
acc.	according to
b.	bar(s)
bt.	beat(s)
corr.	corrected
err.	erroneously
fol.	folio
l.n.	last note
l.s.	lower staff
lv	lower voice
NA	the present edition
p.c.	post correcturam (after correction)
PN	plate number
p.	page
p.i.	parallel instance(s)
r	recto
resp.	respectively
u.s.	upper staff
uv	upper voice
v	verso
pu.n.	penultimate note
→	adapted to

Sources

A   Autograph fair copy of Opp. 90/1–4. 12 folios in landscape format (16 x 24 cm) with 23 written pages. No autograph title on the 1st page, only signature *Fr: Schubert.* in a foreign hand top right. Only scoring *Pianoforte* and numbering *N₽ 1.* in the hand of Franz Schubert on fol. 1r (the autograph scoring recurs on fol. 4r), while the title *Impromptu., Nº 1. in C. moll.* and the publisher's numbers *(5071.)* on fol. 1r (and *(5072.)* on fol. 4r) were added in Tobias Haslinger's hand. At the beginning of Op. 90/3, remark in the hand of Tobias Haslinger: *Im ganzen Takt und in G-Dur um zu schreiben* ('to be transcribed in simple ¢ time and transposed to G major'); corresponding to this, bars 1–4 contain additional bar lines in the middle of the bars.
New York, Pierpont Morgan Library, Music Manuscripts and Printed Music, S384.I34.

Ae   Autograph draft. 8 folios in landscape format (16 x 24,7 cm) with 11 pages written in pencil. Without title and author or tempo indications. The draft comprising 183 bars is complete; its musical text largely corresponds to the final version (only bars 18–33, 180–183 and 192 are lacking)[1].
Vienna, Wienbibliothek im Rathaus, Musiksammlung, MH 145.

EA1   First edition of Opp. 90/1–2 (as *op. 87*) in 2 books by Tobias Haslinger (Vienna 1827). Title: *N₽* [handwritten: *1.* and *2.* resp.] / *Impromptu / pour le / PIANO = FORTE / PAR / Franz Schubert. / OEUVRE 87. / Propriété de l'Editeur / Vienne, chez Tobie Haslinger, / Editeur de Musique / dans la maison de la Caisse d'Epargne, / sur le Graben Nº 572. /* [very faded!] *Jos. List. sc. //.* Heading: *IMPROMPTU.*
Book 1: PN: T. H. 5071.; price: f. 45x C.M./12 gr.
Book 2: PN: T. H. 5072.; price: f. 45x C.M./12 gr.
Copies used: Vienna, Österreichische Nationalbibliothek, Musiksammlung, S.H. Schubert 326 (Op. 90/1) and L 18 Kaldeck M.S. 41118-4°/2 (Op. 90/2).

EA2   First edition of Opp. 90/3–4 in 2 books (numbered as Nos. 3 and 4[2]) by Carl Haslinger (Vienna, 1857). Title: *No.* [stamps: *3* and *4*] / *Impromptu / pour le / PIANO = FORTE / PAR / Franç. Schubert. / OEUVRE 90. / Propriété de l'Editeur / Vienne, chez Charles Haslinger q^m Tobie, / Marchand de Musique etc. de la Cour Imp. et Royale. //*
Book 3: Publisher's catalogue *NEUESTE PIANOFORTE-MUSIK*. PN: (12.075.); price: 45x C.M.
Book 4: PN: (12.076.); price: 45x C.M.
In accordance with Haslinger's entries in **A**, the piece has been transcribed in simple ¢ time (2/2) and transposed to G major in **EA2**. That's why this postumous first edition is only of limited use as a reference source.
Copies used: Vienna, Österreichische Nationalbibliothek, Musiksammlung, S.H. Schubert 334 (book 3); and S.H. Schubert 335 (book 4)[3].

TA   Reissue of the first edition of Opp. 90/1–2 in 2 books by Tobias Haslinger (Vienna, shortly after 1827). Title: *N₽* [handwritten: *1* and *2*] / *Impromptu / pour le / PIANO = FORTE / PAR / Franç. Schubert. / OEUVRE 90. / Propriété de l'Editeur / Vienne, chez Tobie Haslinger, / Editeur de Musique / dans la maison de la Caisse d'Epargne, / sur le Graben Nº 572. //.* Heading: *IMPROMPTU.*
Book 1: PN: T. H. 5071.; price: f. 45x C.M./12 gr.
Book 2: PN: T. H. 5072.; price: f. 45x C.M./12 gr.

---

[1] The draft has been reproduced in *Franz Schubert: Impromptus, Moments musicaux, Drei Klavierstücke. Nach Autographen und Erstdrucken herausgegeben und mit Fingersätzen versehen von Paul Badura-Skoda*, Vienna: Universal Edition, 1969, since 1973 Wiener Urtext Edition, UT 50001, appendix, pp. XXII–XXIX.

[2] At the time the Impromptus Opp. 90/1–2 were engraved again (with the same plate number and page layout); this edition (copies in Vienna, Österreichische Nationalbibliothek, Musiksammlung, S.H. Schubert 328 and S.H. Schubert 332) remains unconsidered here.

[3] Since the copies in the Österreichische Nationalbibliothek in Vienna, S.H. Schubert 333 and S.H. Schubert 334 apparently served for a non-identified later edition, one copy respectively was consulted from a German private collection. This exemplar features the additional publisher indication *Leipsic, chez B. Hermann*.

Copies used: German private possession and Vienna, Österreichische Nationalbibliothek, Musiksammlung, S.H. Schubert 327 (Op. 90/1) and S.H. Schubert 331 (Op. 90/2).

AbN Manuscript copy Noraberg. Copy of Op. 90/1 (probably copied from **EA1**) stemming from the 1st half of the 19th century. 6 folios in portrait format with 12 written pages. Title page: *Impromptu / pour le / Piano-Forte / par / Franz Schubert. //.*
Private possession, last known possessor: Lilly Noraberg, Graz.

AbH Manuscript copy Hölbing. Album of the Hölbing family. 90 folios in landscape format with numerous entries written in the 19th and 20th centuries. Pages 73–77 of the album contain a manuscript copy of Op. 90/3 copied from the autograph; title: *Impromtu* [sic] *von Fr. Schubert*, dated: *Wien am 26. September 1854*. Dedication on p. 77: *Mögen Sie sich zuweilen freundlich erinnern / Ihres aufrichtig ergebenen / Gahy* (probably Josef von Gahy, 1793–1864), underneath entries in the hands of Elly Ney (dated 10 December 1959 and 29 September 1961) and Friedrich Wührer (dated 19 November 1972)[4].
Private possession of the Hölbing family, currently on deposit in the Schubert memorial Atzenbrugg.

AbW Manuscript copy Witteczek-Spaun. Copy of Opp. 90/3 and 4 written by Weiser (first name unknown), the main copyist of the collection Witteczek-Spaun. 10 folios in portrait format with 19 written pages. Author indication: *F: Schubert* on fol. 39r.
Vienna, Gesellschaft der Musikfreunde, Archiv und Bibliothek, Witteczek-Spaun, vol. 60a, fol. 39r–48v.

For the following Detailed Notes the format: bar – staff/voice – symbol in the bar (note, chord or rest) or beat – remark is used.

Impromptu in C minor Op. 90/1 (D 899/1)

Principal source: **A**, reference source: **EA**

Detailed Notes

In **EA** numerous slurs are shorter than in **A**; instead of staccato dots articulation strokes are notated throughout; grace notes notated as small semiquaver (16th) notes in **A** are rendered in **EA** as small crossed-out quavers (8th notes). In **A** and **EA** dottings and triplets have for the most part been assimilated consistently (see also *Notes on Interpretation*).

1f., 9f., 17f., 95f., 103f.	u.s.	bt. 4	**EA**: slur to b. 1, 9, 17, 95 and 103, l.n. only
12–13	u.s.		**A**: slur to b. 12, l.n. only before line break; NA follows **EA**
19	u.s.	1	**EA**: grace notes: ♪ instead of ♫
60			**EA**: *mf* already on u.s., 2nd note
64	l.s.	1–3	**A, EA**: slur 1st–4th note
65			**EA**: *f* not until on bt. 4
73	u.s.		**A**: slur starting between 1st and 2nd notes, **EA**: slur covering 3rd–6th notes only; NA → p.i. b. 52 and 71
75, 76	u.s.		**A**: slur starting between 1st and 2nd notes; NA follows **EA** (cf. also b. 74 and 79ff.)
77	u.s.		**EA**: 2nd slur pu.n. – l.n. only
77			**A**: ⸺ covering 1st and 2nd notes only (with the decrescendo fork starting before 1st note); NA follows **EA**
81	u.s. uv	5–7	**EA**: slur covering pu.n. and l.n. only
97, 98	u.s.		**A**: one slur per bar; NA follows **EA**
104	u.s. uv	3–5	**EA**: slur covering pu.n. and l.n. only
125	u.s.	1	**A**: notehead position very low, pitch may also be read as *c″*
135	u.s.	1	**A**: paper fibre, no staccato dot
154	u.s.		**A**: slur starting between 1st and 2nd notes; NA → p.i. b. 152f. and **EA** (cf. the remark on b. 75, 76)
161	l.s.		**A**: portato on 1st and 2nd notes only, and a subsequent slur covering 3rd–5th notes; NA → p.i. b. 88 and **EA**

Impromptu in E flat major Op. 90/2 (D 899/2)

Principal source: **A**, reference source: **EA**

Detailed Notes

In **A**, the bars 166 and 168 were originally not notated (subsequently inserted with repeat signs and indication *bis*), realised in NA according to **EA** p.c. (there: plate correction). In **A**, bars 169–250, being a repetition of b. 1–82, are not written out, instead their repetition is only indicated by the annotation *D.C. al Segno*; accordingly, after b. 82 Schubert wrote, with regard to b. 251: *Hier folgt beym 2ten Mahl das Coda* ('The 2nd time the Coda follows here'). The concluding bars (b. 277–283) were initially notated on fol. 11r, then crossed out there and repeated almost identical-

---
[4] The album also contains entries referring to Schubert of D 547 (p. 32; Emma Spaun), D 823 (p. 38; Hedwig Hardtmuth) and D 915 (pp. 71–72; Spaun).

ly on fol. 7r (after two additional double sheets had been inserted in the autograph).

1	u.s.		EA: *legato* instead of *ligato*
77 (245)	l.s.	bt. 1	EA: ♪ ᵎ analogous to b. 78f. (= reading of **A** a.c.?, there probably erased and corrected to ♪)
86	l.s.	2	EA: with > (but cf. b. 94)
90, 92	u.s. lv	bt. 3	**A**, **EA** (here also in b. 91): ♪ ᵎ ; NA adapts to the predominant pattern (♪)
111	l.s.	1	**A**: paper fibre, no staccato dot
123			EA: without *p*
168	u.s.	l.n.	EA: without ⌢
184–185			EA: with *cresc.* in b. 184 and *f* on b. 185, 1st note; but cf. b. 16–17
251			EA: without indication *Coda*
279	l.s.	1	**A**: the first transcription on fol. 11r without e♭

Impromptu in G flat major Op. 90/3 (D 899/3)

Principal source: **A**, reference sources: **AbH**, **AbW**

Detailed Notes

EA contains numerous additional dynamics: b. 4, bt. 3: *p*; b. 6, bt. 3+: *cresc.*; b. 8, bt. 1: *p*; b. 31, bt. 1: ⎯⎯; b. 31, bt. 2: ⎯⎯; b. 31, bt. 3: *decresc.*; b. 32, bt. 1: *pp* (instead of in b. 31); b. 47, bt. 3: *decresc.*; b. 52, bt. 3: *cresc.*; b. 57, bt. 2: *cresc.*; b. 58, bt. 3: *p*; b. 60, bt. 4: *cresc.*; b. 62, bt. 1: *p*

5, 59	l.s.	bt. 4	EA: [music example]
11	u./l.s.	1	**A**: ♭ before f♭ and f′♭ missing; added acc. **AbW** (in EA analogously extant)
31		bt. 1	EA: without *pp*
54	l.s.		**A**, **AbW**, **AbH**: err. in halved note values
74	u.s.		EA: ⎯⎯ not until from b. 76
79ff.			EA: without change of key signature

Impromptu in A flat major Op. 90/4 (D 899/4)

Principal source: **A**, reference sources: **EA**, **AbW**

Detailed Notes

In **A**, bars 55–56 are not notated, as repetitions of b. 53–54 they are indicated with a *bis* mark; bars 42 and 66 were inserted later. Bars 171–273, as repetitions of b. 1–102, are not written out in **A**, their repetition is only indicated by *D.C.*; originally the last bars of 90/2 were notated on fol 11r (cf. fol. 7r).

11–12	l.s. lv	2ff.	**AbW**: err. e♭ instead of g♭
23	u./l.s.		**A**, **AbW**, **EA**: slur already from 1st note, in **EA** 1st note additionally with portato dot
25, 27	l.s.		**AbW**: portato already from 1st note; **EA**: b. 25, 1st note with staccato dot
29	u.s.		**A**, **AbW**: portato slur not until from 2nd note; NA → l.s. and **EA**
51, 88	l.s. uv	2	**AbW**: err. without augmentation dot
74–75	u.s.		**AbW**: one slur covering both bars
78, 79	u.s.		**AbW**: one slur per bar
107			EA: without indication *Trio*
116, 118	u.s. uv	2ff.	EA: each note with >
116, 118	l.s. lv	2ff.	EA: each ♪ with >
129	l.s.	2	EA: G♯/B♯/d♯ instead of G♯
149	l.s.	1	**AbW**: Contra-B with additional quarter stem
151	l.s.	1	EA: *D* with additional quarter stem
152	l.s.	3, 5	**AbW**: without additional quarter stem
153	l.s.	3	**AbW**, **EA**: *Contra-A* with additional quarter stem
209–213	l.s.	1	EA: with staccato dot (not, however, at p.i. b. 39–43)
217–233, 250–268	u.s.	9	EA: with staccato dot
268			EA: *ffz* instead of *ff*

WIENER URTEXT EDITION — Klaviermusik

ALBEN
- UT 50250   Expedition Klavier (mit CD)
- UT 50251   Wiener Urtext Album
- UT 50406   From Bach to Schoenberg

J. S. BACH
- UT 50161   Chromatische Fantasie und Fuge BWV 903/903a
- UT 50150   Clavierbüchlein der Anna Magdalena Bach
- UT 50060   Englische Suiten BWV 806–811
- UT 50186   Französische Ouvertüre BWV 831/831a
- UT 50048   Französische Suiten BWV 812–817
- UT 50159   Goldberg-Variationen BWV 988
- UT 50253   Inventionen und Sinfonien BWV 772–801
- UT 50057   Italienisches Konzert BWV 971
- UT 50041   Kleine Präludien und Fughetten
- UT 50192   6 Partiten BWV 825–830
- UT 50081   Toccaten BWV 910–916
- UT 50050/51   Das Wohltemperierte Klavier, Band I, II
- UT 50254   Zweistimmige Inventionen BWV 772–786

BARTÓK
- UT 50411–13   Mikrokosmos, 3 Bände
- UT 50414   Sechs Tänze in Bulgarischem Rhythmus

BEETHOVEN
- UT 50447   Alla ingharese („Die Wuth über den verlornen Groschen") op. 129
- UT 50054   Bagatellen op. 33, op. 119, op. 126
- UT 50425   „Für Elise" WoO 59, Klavierstück „Lustig und Traurig" WoO 54
- UT 50295   Klavierstücke (Neuausgabe)
- UT 50426   Drei Klaviersonaten WoO 47 (Kurfürstensonaten)
- UT 50427–429   Sämtliche Klaviersonaten mit Opuszahl, 3 Bände
- UT 50121   Klaviersonate f-Moll op. 2/1
- UT 50123   Klaviersonate Es-Dur op. 7
- UT 50430   Klaviersonate c-Moll op. 10/1 mit Klavierstücken WoO 52 und 53
- UT 50431   Klaviersonate F-Dur op. 10/2
- UT 50132   Klaviersonate D-Dur op. 10/3
- UT 50435   Klaviersonate c-Moll op. 13 (Grande Sonate pathétique)
- UT 50113   Zwei Klaviersonaten E-Dur/G-Dur op. 14
- UT 50137   Klaviersonate As-Dur op. 26
- UT 50433   Klaviersonate cis-Moll op. 27/2 (Mondscheinsonate)
- UT 50436   Klaviersonate d-Moll op. 31/2
- UT 50248   Zwei Klaviersonaten g-Moll/G-Dur op. 49
- UT 50437   Klaviersonate C-Dur op. 53 und Andante favori WoO 57
- UT 50434   Klaviersonate f-Moll op. 57 (Appassionata)
- UT 50439   Klaviersonate Es-Dur op. 81a (Les Adieux)
- UT 50432   Klaviersonate op. 106 (Hammerklaviersonate)
- UT 50290   Drei Sonatinen für Klavier
- UT 50024/25   Variationen, 2 Bände
- UT 50160/191   Werke für Klavier zu vier Händen, 2 Bände

BRAHMS
- UT 50068   Balladen op. 10
- UT 50072   Fantasien op. 116
- UT 50171   Händel-Variationen op. 24
- UT 50023   3 Intermezzi op. 117
- UT 50102   Klaviersonate op. 1
- UT 50103   Klaviersonate op. 2
- UT 50104   Klaviersonate op. 5
- UT 50067   Klavierstücke op. 76
- UT 50044   Klavierstücke op. 118
- UT 50045   Klavierstücke op. 119
- UT 50172   Paganini-Variationen op. 35
- UT 50007   2 Rhapsodien op. 79
- UT 50231   51 Übungen für das Pianoforte
- UT 50180   Ungarische Tänze, 2hdg.
- UT 50181   Ungarische Tänze, 4hdg.
- UT 50046   Walzer für Klavier op. 39 / Erleichterte Fassung
- UT 50073   Walzer für Klavier op. 39 / Fassung zu 2 Händen
- UT 50074   Walzer für Klavier op. 39 / Fassung zu 4 Händen

BURGMÜLLER
- UT 50130   25 leichte Etüden op. 100

CHOPIN
- UT 50266   Andante spianato und Grande Polonaise brillante op. 22
- UT 50010   Balladen
- UT 50205   Sämtliche Etüden
- UT 50058   Impromptus
- UT 50065   Nocturnes
- UT 50274   Beliebte Nocturnes
- UT 50401   Polonaise As-Dur op. 53
- UT 50157   Polonaisen
- UT 50005   24 Préludes op. 28
- UT 50275   Die leichtesten Préludes
- UT 50061   Scherzi

DEBUSSY
- UT 50083   Deux Arabesques
- UT 50082   Children's Corner
- UT 50291   Clair de lune
- UT 50105/06   Préludes I, II
- UT 50084   Suite bergamasque

HÄNDEL
- UT 50118a/b   Klavierwerke I (Verschiedene Suiten), 2 Bände
- UT 50119   Klavierwerke II (Acht Große Suiten)
- UT 50120   Klavierwerke III (Ausgewählte verschiedene Stücke)

HAYDN
- UT 50077   Andante con variazioni f-Moll Hob. XVII: 6
- UT 50256–59   Sämtliche Klaviersonaten, 4 Bände
- UT 50273   Die leichtesten Klaviersonaten
- UT 50423   Klaviersonate c-Moll Hob. XVI:20
- UT 50403   Klaviersonate A-Dur Hob. XVI:26
- UT 50177   Klaviersonate C-Dur Hob. XVI:35
- UT 50292   Klaviersonate D-Dur Hob. XVI:37
- UT 50424   Klaviersonate C-Dur Hob. XVI:48
- UT 50047   Klavierstücke
- UT 50194   „Il Maestro e lo Scolare" für Klavier vierhändig
- UT 50052   Tänze für Klavier Hob. IX: 3, 8, 11, 12

HINDEMITH
- UT 50128   Ludus tonalis

LISZT
- UT 50165   Consolations
- UT 50233   Etudes d'exécution transcendante mit Grandes Etudes 2 & 7
- UT 50232   Etüden op. 1
- UT 50164   Liebesträume
- UT 50282   Wege zu Franz Liszt

MENDELSSOHN BARTHOLDY
- UT 50075   Lieder ohne Worte
- UT 50215   Rondo capriccioso op. 14
- UT 50278   Variations sérieuses op. 54

MOZART
- UT 50245   Fantasie d-Moll KV 397
- UT 50228   Fantasie und Sonate c-Moll KV 475 und 457
- UT 50418   Klaviersonate A-Dur KV 331 (Neuausgabe)
- UT 50407   Klaviersonate B-Dur KV 570
- UT 50246   Klaviersonate C-Dur KV 545
- UT 50226/27   Klaviersonaten, 2 Bände
- UT 50229/30   Klavierstücke, 2 Bände
- UT 50293   Ouvertüre zu „Die Entführung aus dem Serail" (Klavierfassung)
- UT 50299   Die drei Rondos für Klavier KV 485, 494, 511
- UT 50262   Stücke aus dem Nannerl-Notenbuch
- UT 50096   12 Variationen „Ah, vous dirai-je, Maman" KV 265
- UT 50008/09   Variationen für Klavier, 2 Bände
- UT 50219   Werke für Klavier zu vier Händen

MUSSORGSKI
- UT 50076   Bilder einer Ausstellung

RACHMANINOW
- UT 50417   Prélude cis-Moll op. 3/2

RAVEL
- UT 50261   Gaspard de la nuit
- UT 50265   Menuet sur le nom d'Haydn

SCHÖNBERG
- UT 50195   Ausgewählte Klavierwerke

SCHUBERT
- UT 50294   Die drei Scherzi für Klavier
- UT 50010   Fantasie C-Dur („Wanderer-Fantasie")
- UT 50408   Impromptus D 899 (op. 90)
- UT 50409   Impromptus D 935 (op. post. 142)
- UT 50297   Impromptus, Moments musicaux
- UT 50298   3 Klavierstücke D 946, 2 Fragmente D 916 B/C
- UT 50220–222   Sämtliche Klaviersonaten, 3 Bände
- UT 50196   Klaviersonate A-Dur D 664
- UT 50064   Ländler, Ecossaisen, Menuette
- UT 50410   Moments musicaux D 780 (op. 94)
- UT 50021/22   Sämtliche Tänze für Klavier, 2 Bände
- UT 50063   Walzer und Deutsche Tänze

SCHUMANN
- UT 50271   Ahnung – Albumblatt für Klavier
- UT 50252   Album für die Jugend op. 68 (Neuausgabe)
- UT 50059   Arabeske op. 18, Blumenstück op. 19
- UT 50206   Carnaval op. 9
- UT 50098   Davidsbündlertänze op. 6
- UT 50038   Fantasiestücke op. 12
- UT 50217   Faschingsschwank aus Wien op. 26
- UT 50190   Kinderszenen op. 15 (Neuausgabe)
- UT 50014   Papillons op. 2
- UT 50421   Drei Romanzen op. 28
- UT 50066   Waldszenen op. 82
- UT 50078/79   Sämtliche Werke für Klavier zu vier Händen, 2 Bände

SINDING
- UT 50404   6 Klavierstücke op. 32 (mit „Frühlingsrauschen")

TSCHAIKOWSKY
- UT 50134   Kinderalbum op. 39

Die Reihe wird fortgesetzt / This series will be continued